MY
JOURNEY

MIKE SOCKOL

AuthorHouse™
1663 Liberty Drive
Bloomington, IN 47403
www.authorhouse.com
Phone: 833-262-8899

This book is printed on acid-free paper.

ISBN: 978-1-6655-7812-7 (sc)
ISBN: 978-1-6655-7813-4 (e)

Print information available on the last page.

Published by AuthorHouse 12/15/2022

authorHOUSE®

PROLOGUE

Many five year olds first step through the door of their kindergarten classroom clutching a favorite toy or squeezing a wedge of their blanket. But not Michael. He strode through the open door carrying a book in his arms for he'd taught himself to read by the age of four. And never did he stop. When he turned ten, I bought Mike a complete set of the World Book Encyclopedia. The day they arrived I found him sitting at the kitchen table with Volume One. It was his intent to read through all 22 volumes until I convinced him that was neither necessary nor their purpose. This was the time before the internet, before when needing to know was but finger tips away. Reading was a key to discovery and learning, and learning was Mike's life long passion, particularly learning about history.

He was about six when he created his own little quiz game. Whenever an adult entered the house, Mike would ask, " Please tell me when you were born." The visitor would smile at the youngster and answer with the date. A very short silence would fall, then Mike would tell them who had been President at that time. Sometimes the visitor would ask, "Are you sure?" and Mike would nod his head, but mostly Mike would smile as he walked away.

Another fervor took hold in third grade when Mike found himself on the stage before an audience for the first time. I can't remember the name of the play but I remember vividly how at eight years old Mike lost himself within the character and moved so confidently about the stage of the Hyde Elementary School in Newton. Subsequently, Theater, too, became an integral part of his life. I recall his performance in Once Upon a Mattress when he was in Junior High and his portrayal of Captain Andy in Showboat his senior year at Needham High School.

Upon graduating from Needham High School in 1977, Mike walked through the door of Colgate University, where he continued his life long study of political science and history. There, too, he added yet another passion as a DJ and news director for the campus radio station, WRCU-FM, a fervor so impactful that it seduced him to begin his career not in the academic fields he had excelled at, but as a professional radio broadcaster. For several years, Mike broadcasted throughout the south, Rhode island

and New Hampshire as well as becoming a Television News Reporter for Channel 4 in Port Arthur Texas, where he met his future wife.

I was so deeply thankful each day to modern technology for easy access to Mike's Texas reporting days. I merely typed Mike Sockol Port Arthur Texas into my search bar and Mike appeared, sharing the Channel 4 news of the day with his Texas listeners. How completely professional he is! How competent and charming! To my sorrow, unfortunately, the access stopped after about 3 weeks.

It was probably marriage and fatherhood that convinced Mike to alter his professional path and move with his family back to New England. For five years he worked in the field of public relations for the DeCordova Art Museum in Lincoln, Massachusetts. In the years to follow, his public relations work brought him to Broder Worldwide, and Citicorp, before joining Global Crossing as head of Internal Communications.

To be closer to his work, Mike settled permanently in the picturesque bedroom community of Holmdel, a township of about 18,000 people in Monmouth County, New Jersey.

I suspect it was the birth of his two beloved sons, Matthew and Thomas, that drew Mike to commit time, energy and expertise to addressing the needs of the Town. Or perhaps his innate belief in working for the benefit of others led Mike to served on the Monmouth County Library Commission for two years, and on the Holmdel Board of Education for twelve years, time in which he made a substantial positive impact on the school curriculum, and on addressing the needs of the children and the staff.

Here again, for a brief period, technology enabled me to relive a special event in Mike's life. By simply typing Mike Sockol Holmdel New Jersey into the space bar, I was at the Holmdel High School auditorium as Mike stood before the podium addressing the graduating class of 2014. As if sharing an intimate conversation, Mike looks directly into their faces as he says,

"Always be true to yourself. . . embrace your strengths and address your weaknesses. . . . and remember . . .making friends is more important than making money. Your greatest assets are your family and friends."

He concludes, " Learn to adapt, you never graduate from learning. The world is going to change and you need to change with it. But perhaps my most important piece of advice is to live life fully."

So fruitful were Mike's contributions that The Holmdel Township Committee issued a proclamation signed by Mayor Greg Buontempoo stating among other tributes that, " Whereas, all the residents, parents and students of Holmdel have benefited from Mr. Sockol's generous service to the Township, sincere thanks be given to Mike Sockol for his years of service to the Township." And that, " I do hereby declare September 13th to be Mike Sockol Day in the Township of Holmdel, New Jersey." To be so honored is never to be forgotten.

Always energized and enthused by what he did, Mike's passion for theater lead him to not only continue acting in the New Jersey Community Theater but to write plays. Two of his 30 plays, "Horseshoes" and "Pets", are licensed worldwide and published by Dramatists Play Service, Inc. "Horseshoes" played off broadway at The Thespis Theater Festival in August of 2015.

"Pets" performed by New Jersey theater groups on at least three different occasions, also won Best Original Play, New Jersey Association of Community Theaters in 2018.

Mike's energy seemed almost boundless. Father, head of Internal Communications at a major company, Community service volunteer, Holmdel School Board member, play writer and actor, Mike still found the energy to teach graduate level corporate communications courses at New York University for four years.

Intuitively, Mike knew that the number of years is not the measure of a life. It is the way you live the hours, days, and years that is its measure. And Mike lived his time fully, creating much that will carry on into the future. The vision he brought to the Holmdel School Board will enrich the lives of their students for decades. The wisdom, ideas, perceptions imbedded in his 30 original plays will always spur the thoughts and ideas of others. And though my heart aches to hold him again, to hear his voice and feel his warmth, I know he lives on through his good works and deeds. I know he remains in the hearts and minds of those who knew and loved him.

What follows in the pages ahead are Mike's own words bringing us along with him on his journey through the perilous minefield of Cancer.

Lois Sockol, Mike's Mom

AND THEN THE DOCTOR SAID

In July, 2019, I was diagnosed with stage four pancreatic cancer. I then began a personal log on Facebook, sharing my thoughts and observations along the journey.

JULY 29, 2019

Over the weekend, I put on my old <u>Tiger Schulmann's Red Bank</u> karate T-shirt, traveled to MSK's Middletown clinic, and began my treatments to fight pancreatic cancer.

Fiona just one of the many amazing people I have already encountered at MSK. I'm blessed to have one of the country's best cancer centers only ten minutes from my house.

I know my diagnosis sounds scary, but fortunately, my medical team said my cancer mass is small and that I am an excellent candidate for new treatments that have shown success in shrinking tumors like mine.

My sense of humor remains intact. I did get a few knowledgable chuckles when I asked the medical team that put in a "port" in my chest to receive chemo if that means I can also now charge "tariffs" for Chinese medicine.

I feel good--both mentally and physically--and with the support of friends and family, I look forward to adding new accomplishment to my resume--cancer survivor.

Carpe die

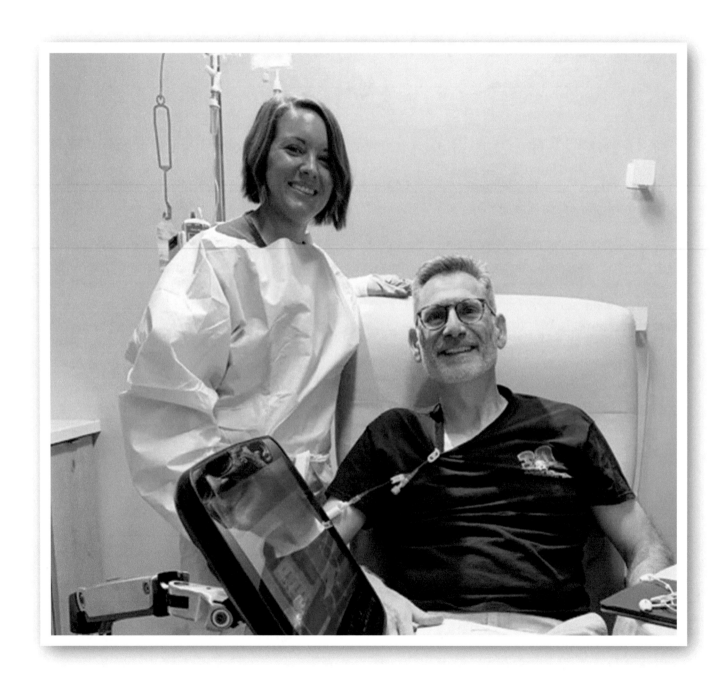

AUGUST 1, 2019

Wow.

I'm simply overwhelmed by the response I have received on Facebook. Mindblowing in fact. The journey begins and it's nice to see so many people riding in the backseat. Just don't ask if we're there yet.

Sammi, my nurse practitioner, will deliver her first child later this month. No circle of life references, please. I already promised that I would be around when she returns from maternity leave. She concurred.

Today was my first follow-up visit after starting chemo. So far, the side effects haven't been too bad. A little nausea, but controllable by meds, and few more naps than usual, but no pain and remain in good spirits.

Appetite remains good, too. In fact, I am finding that MSK has very tasty Graham Crackers....

AUGUST 11, 2019

The lovely Georgia and Laura, who assisted me Saturday in receiving my second round of chemo, with the addition of a pretty nasty new drug that immediately made its presence known. Severe nausea all day, but I don't blame the new medication. I blame my decision to have a smoothie in the morning that simply did not digest. Good lesson for me as we continue down this path. A lot of vomiting, but after shifting my diet to crackers and ginger tea (as well as ginger ale), I am feeling a little better. As I have mentioned to friends, it's my job to focus on the things I can control—-what I eat, how I exercise, getting the most of our every day, and maintaining a good mental **attitude. Everything else isn't worth worrying about. Except maybe worrying about losing my hair.**

Oh, by the way, I wasn't going to let a little thing like a chemo treatment keep me away from supporting the Monmouth Film Festival and to participate in tonight's awards ceremony. Thanks to the Marcheses for asking me to co-host this event. It's always a blast. The action starts about 30 minutes into the video. Osu!

AUGUST 24, 2019

Meet Nino, my new friend from Georgia (the place the Beatles sang about in "Back in the USSR"), a very efficient nurse who managed my treatment today (including the anti-nausea drugs they forgot to include in the second round). Already feeling much better than the second round, which is a real positive. Let's see how the next couple of days go.

Last week was positive and energetic--going to concerts, taking an acting class, meeting old friends in New York. And then doing something truly daring--auditioning for a role I really wanted--cancer be damned.

So, today, Circle Players announced I have been cast in their production of "Seminar" as Leonard. Miraculous as that might be, I was floored when the director told me that he already knew I had cancer (after I shared that information with him). He didn't let my illness impact his casting decision.

It is refreshing to find people who focus on the positives and possibilities, and not dwell on the negatives or what might happen. I won't let cancer define me or what I do. Because that's the only way cancer can beat me.

SEPTEMBER 5, 2019

As I was walking in NYC Wednesday, I saw a homeless man with a sign saying that he had pancreatic cancer and that he was terminal. So I asked him to tell me his story. He left his job, failed to sign up for health insurance, fell off a ladder and broke his back. While hospitalized, he learned he had cancer, which went into remission, and now it had returned. He expected to die in three months because he wasn't going to go back for treatment.

I was a little skeptical about his story. When I told him I had pancreatic cancer, the guilty look on his face gave away the lie. But it didn't matter. I gave him some money anyway and hopefully some advice that was more valuable. "You have a choice," I told him. "Choose life."

SEPTEMBER 5, 2019

Round four begins with blood testing, and surprise, surprise, the lovely Lauren is on hand to access my port and get all those vital fluids. Considering the size of the MSG lab team, it is somewhat amazing that Lauren keeps getting my number, often drawing blood or disconnecting my empty bag from my port. I'm the lucky one. She's a real professional, and she's always inquisitive about how and what I'm doing. And she wants to see "Pets and Their Humans" at the First Avenue Theater (if someone would just pick up the phone. :)

The chemo is a basically scrambling my taste buds. Nothing tastes the same, so I'm wondering if this is finally the time to try liver.....

A good meeting with my doctor before chemo. He wants to conduct a follow-up screen in two weeks. He also said I look good, but then I still have more hair than he does.

Stay well. Enjoy the day.

SEPTEMBER 19, 2019

Dr. Ilson is my oncologist here at Memorial Sloan Kettering, which means in simple terms, he's the guy working to extend my life. He had some good news to share with me today. My latest scan shows that the pancreatic tumor has shrunk about 30 percent, and my malignant lesions in my liver are declining, too. Still a long road ahead, so best to stay even keel about this, but when you have a doctor almost acting happier than you, than that's probably the best sign of all.

OCTOBER 5, 2019

Round six began on Thursday (sure sounds like a boxing match by now, doesn't?). Let me introduce you to two other members of the growing Sockol team, Melanie and Alvin, who was running the nursing operations on Thursday at MSK (he also handled my chemo two weeks ago). Even when I fell asleep in the chair, Melanie deftly switched medicine bags without waking me up.

They seemed pleased enough with my current health that they gave me a flu shot. And they are going to let my dentist clean my teeth. My red and white blood cells are putting up quite a fight. And my weight remains steady after 12 weeks of treatment.

Fitting that this round of chemo took place in the middle of the holiest week of the Jewish New Year, the time between Rosh Hashana and Yom Kippur when we pray for good health and a favorable spot on the Book of Life. This is the week God listens--not to who prays the loudest, but those who pray with sincerity and forgiveness. When my rabbi stopped by to deliver his wife's homemade honey bread (and a delicious gift indeed), I told him about my diagnosis, and he didn't skip a beat in his response--God only gives out challenges to those that can handle them.

So who am I to argue with God?

OCTOBER 17, 2019

Okay, first don't get me wrong. Cancer sucks. No denying that. But there are plenty of ways to fight back. For example, for the last month and a half, I have made it a practice of going to the gym and working out on the days that I get chemo treatments. Today was round 7, so here I am beforehand, getting all those white and red blood cells pumped up for battle. Biceps, triceps, hip

flexors, shoulders, and abdominal workouts followed by 20 to 30 minutes on the elliptical machine. Sadly, I can't do much with chest muscles, because I might accidentally move the port the surgeon put in there. But do have a pretty sexy scar.

NOVEMBER 1, 2019

Chemo round 8 took place on Halloween. Luckily, no one chose to dress up like zombies, but my nurses Nicole and Megan did get into the spirit of the day. This latest round of chemo came during a perfect storm of demands on my time. I'm on the home stretch for two time-consuming activities--my re-election campaign for school board and my pending performance in "Seminar." On top of that, it has been a particularly busy time for work--three clients wanting stuff simultaneously. Nothing like writing a press release an hour after you get your chemo.

Cancer has been quite an adventure. For example, I failed my first urine test the other day, which I needed for a background check from a new client. Since the medical team at MSK has practically turned my body into a chemistry set, the outcome was no surprise. Still, it was a little fun to tell the worried inspector that I wasn't smoking marijuana but taking a drug that contained HTC to help with my appetite. A quick call to the pharmacist squared things up.

This is my new normal. Trying to balance the normalcy of work and play without letting cancer get in the way (the rhyme is accidental, but could still make a good song lyric). The best lesson from all of this--don't take the good days for granted. Make the most of them. And thanks everyone for your prayers

and support. I don't say thanks enough!

NOVEMBER 15, 2019

November is Pancreatic Cancer Awareness Month, so it's fitting that I would get my own personal awareness when I received my latest cancer scan this week. Before I share the results, let me also offer a few important data points. Almost every website out there will tell you that stage four pancreatic cancer is essentially incurable. Even today, the one-year survival rate for pancreatic cancer is only 20%. Less than 10% of pancreatic cancer patients make it to five years. In fact, most pancreatic cancer patients die within six months after diagnosis.

Pretty sobering, huh.

I learned on Thursday that my pancreatic tumor has shrunk 75% since I began treatment five months ago (it is about the size of my thumbnail). The largest lesion in my liver is almost gone. Even the body language of my seasoned oncologist betrayed his giddiness. So, yes, you can say that Thanksgiving Day will have special meaning for me this year.

All of this must be taken with a grain of salt. There is a lot more fighting to do. But there is one blessing. I have really come to appreciate the "good" days when I feel almost normal again. Make sure you make the most of yours.

And show your real colors. Wear purple. Thanks.

NOVEMBER 17, 2019

Years ago, when I was training for my black belt, my Sensei, <u>Jason Hoffman</u>, who still remains one of the most influential people in my life, told the class that the things you value the most are the things you have to work the hardest to get.

So true.

Shortly after my diagnosis, I made a bet on myself. I knew the depressing statistics on survival rates and the long odds I faced. But I had circled (no pun intended) the date for Circle Players production of Seminar months before. I wanted to play Leonard, a true dream role, and much to my surprise, I was cast.

That was frankly a miracle, but even more miraculous has been the love and support that has been shown by the wonderful cast and crew, including <u>Matt Lafargue</u>(Director), <u>Casey Okamoto</u> (Stage Manager), <u>Faith Dowgin</u> (Producer), <u>Kelly Kline</u>, <u>Megan Whitehead</u>, <u>Garrett John</u>, and <u>Michael McEntee</u>.

I also want to also give a quick nod to my amazing friend and teacher, <u>Jared Kelner</u>, whose lessons (and passion) around acting have been an amazing influence as well. Being both an actor and a trained martial artist has come in handy throughout the rehearsal process. For instance, our first tech day was particularly difficult, coming on the heels of my latest chemo treatment. Nauseous, dizzy, and physically exhausted, I still plowed through monologue after monologue, before slinking back home and crashing into bed for a three-hour nap.

Sometimes that's the price you pay to get something you really truly want. I'll be fine once the lights go up. Trust me.

Seminar's three-week run begins next week. Come and see it because you will be entertained. Or possibly, for those of you who have been following my posts, even inspired. Thanks.

NOVEMBER 28, 2019

Thanksgiving should be seen as a celebration of families and friends. But in recent months, I have found that definition to be a little limiting. I'm thankful for the researchers who spend countless hours seeking new cures for cancer. I'm thankful for my medical team and the progress they have made in my own case. I'm thankful for the remarkable support and prayers I have received these last few months from so many people.Most of all, I'm thankful I'm here today to write this message.

On Black Friday, take a few moments to find peace and healing by joining my wife for her special yoga class dedicated to raise awareness of pancreatic cancer.

Happy Turkey Day everyone.

DECEMBER 2, 2019

The tenth round of chemo today, completing almost a half year of treatment. To be honest, not a pleasant day, complete with vomiting and tingling fingers. But rather than tantalize everyone with more pictures of pretty nurses, I would rather focus instead on an unusual coincidence that will begin tragically, but hopefully will end on an optimistic note.

Alan Rickman, a brilliant actor who was diagnosed with Stage Four pancreatic cancer and died six months later in 2016. Here's the irony. Six months after my diagnosis, I'm playing "Leonard," the part Rickman originated during the original Broadway run of "Seminar." This Circle Players, Inc.'s production comes to an end this weekend up in Piscataway (get your tickets soon, ok?) Just another sign of how much progress medical research has made in just the last few years. As you fight through a cancer diagnosis, you remember all the patients who fought just as hard as you. Some make it. Some don't. Most of them worked very hard not to let cancer define their lives. Most of them are not as famous as Alan Rickman or Alex Trebek or Ruth Bader Ginsberg. But that doesn't mean they don't deserve to be remembered or honored.

My last three performances are dedicated to Alan Rickman (and others like him who left the world's "stage" too soon). Not because we share the same terrible disease, but because we both shared a similar joy for theater, and I feel an obligation to carry that spirit forward. I hope you will join me and our marvelous cast and crew for what will be three very special and personal performances for me. Friday and Saturday at 8 p.m and Sunday at 3 p.m.

Happy holidays, everyone. Feel free to share this note.

DECEMBER 5, 2019

"You beat cancer by how you live, why you live, and in the manner in which you live."

I remember the ESPY awards ceremony when Stuart Scott said those words. It was a gutsy way to look at how we all should face adversity.

The secret is to translate the words into action. One personal example takes place this weekend as I perform in the final three shows of <u>Circle Players, Inc.</u>'s production of "Seminar." Friday and Saturday at 8 pm and Sunday at 3 pm.

It will be a pretty special moment for me. I hope we can share it together.

DECEMBER 23, 2019

A few days after my latest round of chemo last week (provided by the lovely duo of Jen and Laura), I had a chance to catch up with several of Lisa's cousins at a holiday gathering at her aunt's apartment in Greenwich Village. Robin is a cancer survivor, and she introduced me to two of her friends, who are cancer survivors themselves. Then they pointed to me, and said, "You're a cancer survivor, too." Woah. Talk about crossing a medical Rubican. I recognize that I have made steady progress in my treatment. I generally feel pretty good (with a disclaimer that seems to delight my brothers--"for my age"), but unlike one of my old bosses, I don't delight in prematurely declaring victory. I will take my "wins" on a day to day basis for the time being.

But all this talk about being a survivor made me think

a little a bit about what I have survived so far--adulthood, friendship, work, marriage, and parenting, just to name a few. Doing the practical and the necessary (working to pay my bills) while balancing an ongoing effort to challenge myself (the improbable, successful obtainment of a black belt in martial arts). Or maybe savoring moments of good fortune while deflecting the unfairness of life that seems to creep up when you least expect it.

In other words, life is not about surviving cancer or another disease. Life is about surviving life. With a new decade before us, being a "life survivor" would suit me just fine.

JANUARY 3, 2020

And why not some Jewish folk wisdom to start the new year, courtesy of a book my Mom is currently reading.

- Moses said, " The law is everything."
- Jesus said, " Love is everything."
- Marx said, " Money is everything."
- Freud said, " Sex is everything."
- Einstein said, " Everything is relative."

Of course, I might add one more--luck. I could have "everything" on this list, but unfortunately, pancreatic cancer doesn't have a sense of humor.

I began my first round of chemo of the year on January 2 (the first of three this month, but I couldn't sell MSK on the idea of a 3 for 2 special), and I can't look back at 2019 and not feel lucky and thankful:

1. Over the last six months, I have made great progress with a treatment that only has a 40% success rate.
2. I have been able to work and do almost everything I want to.
3. It was a narrow margin, but I'm so thankful that so many people in Holmdel value my public service and want me to remain on the Township School Board.
4. The response I have received from family and friends is beyond describing. I'm certain God and his administrative staff are having a tough time processing all the prayers.

So I chose to post <u>this short video</u> on Lou Gehring's final appearance at Yankee Stadium. When I was a baseball-fanatic pre-teen, I used to read everything I could find about the game, and when I read Lou Gehring's story I was confused. Why would a ballplayer still in his prime tell everyone he was the "luckiest man on the face of the earth" when he was about to die from a disease that bore his name?

Now, I understand. We should not need a "life-defining" event to take a moment to take stock of what we have accomplished in own lives or whose lives we have touched. Being lucky is doing the right thing as often as we can. Being lucky is about getting satisfaction from seizing opportunities or trying things that seem absurd or even dangerous. If that means creating a bucket list, that fine. But don't forget the simple things that come from being kind, empathetic, and patient with fellow human beings. Those are good things to base your resolutions on. Being lucky is part of living, which is probably why Gehrig closed his remarks by saying that he still "had a lot to live for."

I might add, so do I.

With much love, Happy New Year everyone.

JANUARY 7, 2020

Years ago, I watched a Twilight Zone episode ("A Matter of Minutes") in which a husband and wife fall out of sync with time. The story suggested that a small army of workers rebuilds every moment in time from scratch. Because they are now in "limbo" they are forced to join this work gang for eternity, but they manage to escape and "jump" back into the right time sequence and return to their normal life.

I love this allegory. Life should be viewed as a series of separate parts, knitted together, but individual in its own way, each component worthy of your time and attention. How many sequences to do we allow to slip away? Probably too many.

Our lives are being built, piece by piece, by an army of people, some visible, some invisible. Usually, we are active participants, but too often we aren't. The stream of time flows forever, but the journey upon it is short and undefined.

Warren Zevon was dying of cancer when he made his last appearance on the David Letterman show. His parting advice was simple but powerful--"Enjoy every sandwich."

Make mine a Reuben.

JANUARY 31, 2020

Marie, my CAT scan technician,wouldn't stop laughing when I started to sing "CAT scan" to the Batman theme. Honestly, they let cancer patients get away with anything these days....

A lot of smiles Thursday at MSK. The latest scan was pretty good. They can't see the cancer anymore in my liver, and the pancreatic tumor continues to shrink, almost 90% since last summer. My doctor feels I'm exceeding expectations and we will keep those chemo appointments for the time being. Overall, I feel pretty good. Yet, more progress is necessary before declaring victory. Onward.

A lot of people come up to me and say they admire my positive attitude. Well, let me share a little secret. I'm a super competitive person (that could have started when me and my three brothers sat at the dinner table quickly grabbing food before it was gone). Let me give you an example. Throughout treatment, I have actually pushed myself to see how much I could eat, despite the nausea. It wasn't always fun, but gradually, my body started getting the message.

I can get easily bored without challenges. I guess God wanted to see what would happen if he threw a challenge at me for all the marbles.

And that maybe one of the reasons why I found "The Good Place" so appealing. I don't want to give away any spoilers now that the show has reached one of the most satisfying conclusions I have seen. The show was grounded on eye-opening philosophical and theological notions that tackle the most challenging moral issues of all. In a beautiful dance, four misguided humans and a reformed demon asked big questions and more. I'll be thinking about Chidi's Buddist "wave" analogy for a very long time (no more details from last night's finale, trust me).

Maybe we shouldn't have eaten from the tree of knowledge, and life might have been happier if we hadn't been kicked out Eden (the original Brexit, perhaps), but I don't think so. We are restless, thinking creatures, and it is healthy for us to ask the fundamental questions of why belong, what is our role in the universe, why is there an "end," and why would the Great Creator put mosquitos on the earth in the first place?

I do get teased a lot because I like to assume positive intent in others. It doesn't mean I'm not a skeptic or cynic (just listen to the Impeachment hearings). But we need to give people permission to ask big questions. Who will win the Super Bowl? Who is your favorite candidate for president? Will I really be healthy if I eat the Impossible Whopper? The important thing is that we need to give ourselves permission to listen openly to the answers, even when we don't disagree.

I don't ask God why I have cancer. We just keep our discussion on more important topics--like how I should live. I expect that conversation to continue a little while longer.

FEBRUARY 1, 2020

A lot of smiles Thursday at MSK. The latest scan was pretty good. They can't see the cancer anymore in my liver, and the pancreatic tumor continues to shrink, almost 90% since last summer. My doctor feels I'm exceeding expectations and we will keep those chemo appointments for the time being. Overall, I feel pretty good. Yet, more progress is necessary before declaring victory. Onward.

A lot of people come up to me and say they admire my positive attitude. Well, let me share a little secret. I'm a super competitive person (that could have started when me and my three brothers sat at the dinner table quickly grabbing food before it was gone). Let me give you an example. Throughout treatment, I have actually pushed myself to see how much I could eat, despite the nausea. It wasn't always fun, but gradually, my body started getting the message.

I can get easily bored without challenges. I guess God wanted to see what would happen if he threw a challenge at me for all the marbles.

And that maybe one of the reasons why I found "The Good Place" so appealing. I don't want to give away any spoilers now that the show has reached one of the most satisfying conclusions I have seen. The show was grounded on eye-opening philosophical and theological notions that tackle the most challenging moral issues of all. In a beautiful dance, four misguided humans and a reformed demon asked big questions and more. I'll be thinking about Chidi's Buddist "wave" analogy for a very long time (no more details from last night's finale, trust me).

Maybe we shouldn't have eaten from the tree of knowledge, and life might have been happier if we hadn't been kicked out Eden (the original Brexit, perhaps), but I don't think so. We are restless, thinking creatures, and it is healthy for us to ask the fundamental questions of why belong, what is our role in the universe, why is there an "end," and why would the Great Creator put mosquitos on the earth in the first place?

I do get teased a lot because I like to assume positive intent in others. It doesn't mean I'm not a skeptic or cynic (just listen to the Impeachment hearings). But we need to give people permission to ask big questions. Who will win the Super Bowl? Who is your favorite candidate for president? Will I really be healthy if I eat the Impossible Whopper? The important thing is that we need to give ourselves permission to listen openly to the answers, even when we don't disagree.

I don't ask God why I have cancer. We just keep our discussion on more important topics--like how I should live. I expect that conversation to continue a little while longer.

MARCH 7, 2020

I have been busy. "Harvey" goes live in two weeks at Playhouse 22, and auditions take place in a few days for "In Danger of Falling in Love," a play I wrote that will debut in May at Villagers. My latest play, "Big in Texas," will debut in another festival in June, and I'll have start casting that as well. In between, I plan to head back to Colgate for a reunion of the school's radio station. My business clients love my work (so far) and the first two months of my tenure as Vice President of the School Board has been filled with meetings and emails. I feel pretty good, almost good enough to forget this malignant tumor less than the size of a thumbnail lurking inside of me.

Well, not quite, sports fans.

Of course, it's always a good sign when you have an oncologist who smiles every time he sees me and a medical staff trying to keep their enthusiasm contained with professional straight faces. My doctor suggested last week that I'm in partial remission, a term I would equate to being almost pregnant, but I'll take it. After eight months of chemo, I guess I earned any amount of optimism he wants to throw my way. That's Lauren, by the way, giving a thumbs up after giving me my latest treatment.

And then came this little virus called Covid.

I understand a lot of people are worried, even a little scared. Panic floats in the air like a black balloon. It reminds me of a George Carlin routine in which he talked about swimming in the East River as a kid to build up an immunity system that can stop anything. Maybe he has a point. Or maybe we have to let the math play out, which even in a worse case scenario, suggests that 96 to 98 percent of us who get the flu will be all right. At least I know my white blood cells are battle tested already.

My wife teases me that she doesn't know where all my energy comes from. I think it comes from a relentless desire to just enjoy life while I can. Something will get me eventually. I just plan to put up a pretty good fight in the process.

Stay well everyone. And keep washing your hands.

MARCH 28, 2020

Today is one of my favorite days--disconnect day. As some of you know every, two weeks, I take some of my chemo home with me in a fanny pack attached to a port in my chest. Two days later I return to MSK, and they unplug me. They keep asking me if I want to take it out myself, but I'll defer to trained nurses like Brigit here. You'll notice we were practicing a "social distancing" selfie...

These days, we are all disconnecting in someway. Living in a time of plague does that to you. So many things that I enjoy have been taken from me in recent weeks, the things that help keep my mind on other stuff besides my condition. I get more worried calls these days. The chemo does depress my immune system, but my white blood cells are hardy little suckers, and seem to keep bouncing back. I'm careful about where I go, and I wash my hands religiously. I'm really doing pretty well and have much fewer side effects since they cut my regimen from three chemo drugs to two. Somehow, I don't think God would have had me go through 9 months of chemo just to kill me with a virus. He may have dark sense of humor about things, but not that dark.

And so, you restart that old discussion about fate, the things you can control and those you can't. The strategy of my current treatment is pretty simple. How many more good days can my doctors squeeze out of my life? And will I make the most of each and every one of them. It's a question we should all ask ourselves. I may have fewer than most people, not just because I have cancer, but simply because I'm older. Or maybe it's not that simple. A younger person may have more "good" days than me, but is he or she taking advantage of that surplus--sort of a variation of that old saying that youth is wasted on the young.

So now, I need to redefine good days. I'm lucky that I can work remotely. I'm lucky I get treatment ten minutes from my house. I'm lucky to have a dog that wants company and gives me an excuse to take him for a walk (at least when it isn't raining). I'm lucky to have family and friends who challenge me to stay active.

Rick and Ilsa had Paris. I have Zoom. Less romantic, but practical just the same.

Stanford psychology professor Jamil Zaki believes the current crisis is unleashing the good qualities of humans beings--more altruism as we replace the fallacy of self reliance with our natural proclivities to help others in times of need. Professor Zaki believes we are experiencing two global epidemics at the moment--one is viral, while the other is built upon kindness.

There are two statistical numbers that give me the perspective that I need right now.--2% and 80%. Both represent projected mortality rates. Roughly 2% of coronavirus patients are dying right now. But for those who have stage four pancreatic cancer, the mortality rate for a 12 month period is 80%. I've had my "come to Jesus" discussion with God already, and the conclusion is unmistakable. I haven't come this far to allow other health threats disrupt my ability to enjoy the good days. At some point this contagion may diminish, but the threat will continue to hang over all of us. When it is time to go outside again, I will put risk aside. There is no fun living in a hermetically sealed bubble.

Stay healthy. Keep your hands off your face. And wash those hands. We'll all get through this together.

APRIL 6, 2020

A pandemic reaches our shores from Asia. A top health official urges public officials to contain the disease, but business and government leaders resist calls for a quarantine and try to downplay the threat for economic reasons. They claim health officials are exaggerating the threat, even spreading fake news.

Sound familiar? It actually happened more than a hundred years ago, when rats carrying bubonic plague on board an Asian steamship arrived in San Fransisco around 1900.

The doctor who first sounded the alarm, Dr. Joseph J. Kinyoun, is commonly known as the father of the National Institutes of Health and an early proponent of using microscopes to study bacteria. One of his enemies? Levi Strauss (you may be wearing one of his jeans right now), who called Dr. Kinyoun a fake. The California government managed to get rid of Dr. Kinyoun by requesting his transfer to a federal facility in Michigan. His successor did a better job convincing officials that they needed to turn their attention on controlling the rat population. But because of their failure to act quickly, it took officials almost eight years before they contained the epidemic.

By the way, the first major pandemic of recorded history happened during the reign of Justinian in the sixth century, when the source bacteria of bubonic plague made its first appearance in Europe, and conservatively wiped out between 15 to 25% of the population. Some historians think the rapid loss of so much ancient knowledge triggered the Dark Ages in the West.

I believe pandemics are just God's way of reminding us of our own hubris.

Nine months of chemo, on the other hand, has a way of making you humble and appreciative of every good day you get. For me, the coronavirus is more of a mental challenge than a physical one. I'm too competitive to cede the battlefield to a virus when I need to focus my energies towards addressing an adversary just as stubborn as I am.

Coaches give pep talks to rally their teams. One of my new habits involve periodic mental pep talks to my white blood cells. I tell them how important they are and how I'm counting on them to win the fight. MSK has provided me with this cool chart, tracking progress over the past year. When I first started receiving chemo treatments, those white blood cells got beaten up pretty badly. But in the last few months, they have been on the upswing, almost as if they got a second wind.

Justinian must have had good white blood cells, too, because he was infected by the plague, but survived. I'd like to think his all-consuming focus on reuniting the Roman Empire also gave him a mental edge--a boost of positive energy that even the plague could not overcome. He had a vision of something great, and he wasn't going to let something like a pandemic get in the way.

We have made great progress since the days of Justinian. It might be difficult these days to find Lysol wipes, but at least we aren't sharing our food with rats anymore (or at least not usually). The biggest challenge facing us isn't really boredom. It's finding a way to make the most of the good days we have. And keeping our hands clean in the process.

STAY
HEALTHY, HELPFUL, HAPPY

AND CALM

APRIL 8, 2020

We live in a strange time when almost everything we do seems to come down to being a "life or death" decision. It is an odd feeling that you don't usually experience in so-called civilized societies (although there hundreds of thousands of people around the world who life in dystopic societies in which every day is a struggle to survive).

Dying to have a milkshake from McDonalds takes on new meaning in the age of coronavirus.

But sometimes these "tough decisions" turn out to be less "tough" than we imagine. So it was that my doctor, concerned about the rising number of coronavirus cases in New Jersey, suggested that maybe we should spread out my "treatments," under the overall assumption that I'm doing well and that I should try to limit my trips to the clinic.

Naturally, I appreciate the concern. At the same time, I believe I'm doing "well" because of my current treatment schedule. To disrupt the "known" because of a threat from the "unknown" makes no sense to me. I can try to control risk by taking precautions (masks and gloves) but I can't eliminate it. And what happens if I don't get the coronavirus, but my tumor gains new momentum and starts growing again? It is a decision ripe with lethal consequences.

So we compromised. I noted that Saturdays are low traffic days in Monmouth, and I suggested we shift the day of the week for my chemo, rather than extending out the treatments from every two weeks to three. And he agreed.

I believe social distancing is important. I believe staying home-bound as much as possible is important. I also believe in my own common sense. It doesn't always win out in the end, but I think this time it did.

APRIL 11, 2020

The nausea has a bit of a bite today following chemo. A little tired too. But I still find ways to rev up my appetite.

I do have some traditional tastes. Must come from my love of history. What I wouldn't give to eat a Gros Michel bananna, for example, which were killed off by its own version of the coronavirus in the 1950s. I understand they still grow small quantities somewhere in Asia.

I also like chocolate sandwich cookies. Oreos naturally dominate the market, and I realize there are some alternate brands out there, but nothing beats my childhood experience of eating Sunshine Hydrox cookies (their raisin biscuits were heavenly too. The cookie that I could completely demolish out of the pack in one sitting, much to the dismay of my mother).

Unfortunately, Sunshine sold its brand to Keebler in the mid 1990s, and few years later, they gave up making them, except in 2008, when Kellogg (which bought Keebler) introduced it on its 100th anniversary for a few months.

I like Hydrox cookies. They have a distinctly different taste. Less artificial. The cocoa flavor nicely balances the cream filling. When I learned I could buy them from Amazon, I ordered a box. Sadly, they arrived today.

Sadly? I am following my Passover routine. I can't touch them until after the holiday period ends. God is testing me again. So now I face the greatest of temptation. A box mutely mocks me less than six feet away. When it comes to Hydrox, no social distancing necessary.

Sigh,

MAY 30, 2020

When I was in sixth grade, students from all of the local elementary schools gathered for a track and field day. We were all assigned specific events. For some reason, I ended up running the 400 meter race. When the gun went off, I took off like a shot, and at the 200 meter mark, I was in the lead. But I had never run a long distance race before. I quickly ran out of "gas," and finished last. But I always remember one of the teachers encouraging me to finish strong and folks in the crowd complimenting me for my "closing kick."

Last summer, around my 60th birthday, I learned I had stage four pancreatic cancer. In the weeks before my official diagnosis, I began doing a little research. Every medical web site I visited said the same thing. I had a terminal disease. Chemotherapy would only be palliative. Most patients with my condition were dead in six months.

I want to emphasis the world "every." There was not one glimmer of hope. Not one piece of research to suggest any other outcome. Even my oncologist refused to say how long I had to live. He saw treatment as a year to year process. He thought I was a good candidate for a new treatment that showed progress--three chemo drugs that he euphemistically called a "spicy cocktail." But even that treatment failed for most patients.

So I was left with only one real option. No matter what was going to happen, I was going to make sure I had a strong closing kick.

I kept working, even flying to New Orleans to run a major off-site event for a client one day after treatment. I auditioned and won a dream role in a local theater production. I wrote and rewrote plays. I successfully ran for another term for school board. I made sure I made the most of every good day I had. And every bad one, too.

Taking three chemo drugs was hard, but how can you seriously complain about a treatment designed to give you a chance?

Today, I feel great. My doctor uses terms like "partial" remission. I'm on two chemo drugs now and my blood work, including my white blood cells, are essentially normal. My antigen marker that signals my type of cancer continues to drop. The neuropathy in my feet is beginning to fade. Knock on wood, but there is some degree of hope that I will make it to my 61st birthday next month. Or at least see the rest of season three of "Ozark."

I'm not out of the woods. I expect to be fighting cancer for the rest of my life. But I also know it can't actually beat me. Not as long as I have a strong closing kick.

JUNE 3, 2020

Shortly after I got my cancer diagnosis last summer, I made a conscious decision to be as irrelevant as possible in my interactions with the staff at MSK. After all, I suspect most of the time, their days are filled with pretty depressing stuff, so they can use some levity. So whenever I call my doctor, I try to make his receptionist laugh, usually with pretty bad jokes. When I get calls from the medical staff to remind me of my chemo appointments, I make sure I tell them how "fired up" I am and how much my body really loves these treatments without any hint of sarcasm. And every few months, when I get a CAT scan to track the progress of my treatment, I usually crack up the technicians with my rendition of "CAT Scan" sung to the tune of the TV show, Batman.

So as I prepare for this week's chemo treatment, I can at least feel good about the CAT scan results I received this week. The tumor in my pancreas has shrunk by 92% since treatment began last July, and the liver remains clear of the malignant lesions that were spotted during my first scan. It's also a good sign when your oncologist smiles a lot. Or when you have more hair than he does.

Meanwhile, the MSK staff should get a little worried about the direction of all this "entertainment" I'm providing. I just got a ukulele.

JULY 5, 2020

I was attending a neighborhood Fourth of July party last year, when I received the first indication that I had a growth on my pancreas and spots on my liver. I didn't need a biopsy to know what it meant, and suddenly I found myself declaring my independence from a lot of things I had taken for granted.

I don't know why, but one of the first things that popped into my mind was a promise I made to myself.

As far as I'm concerned, there is no better whiskey in the world than Johnnie Walker Blue Label Scotch. Three fingers. Two ice cubes. One hour of contented sipping. So, I guess I'm not really surprised that I told myself that if I managed to make it to another Fourth of July party, I was going to buy a bottle of Johnnie Walker Blue to celebrate.

When I learned that a few of our neighbors planned to gather despite our global pandemic, I put my plan into action. We sat around a pool, cooked hamburgers and hot dogs, maintained proper social distancing, and enjoyed an impromptu fireworks display. In between, we all sampled one of the smoothest Scotch whiskeys you can buy. A new tradition had been born.

Thank you for all the kind wishes I recently received for my birthday. Now you all know the perfect gift when I celebrate my birthday next year as well (although I will always settle for a package of Hydrox cookies). Some of my more optimistic friends have already suggested I should just go ahead and buy myself a case.

Cheers.

JULY 26, 2020

This week marks my first year of chemotherapy. The scar where they put in the port in my chest for my transfusions is barely noticeable now, and the folks at MSK Monmouth pretty much know me as this relentlessly cheerful guy who dances in the lobby area on the days they disconnect me from the chemo pouch I carry around for two days.

When I began my treatments, I asked my doctor about my prognosis. He said with a cancer like mine, it's best to take it year by year, with the understanding that once one treatment runs its course, hopefully something new in the pipeline will take its place.

So far, my treatment has gone fine. To put it bluntly, modern medicine gave me another year to live. It's a good moment to assess what I did with all that extra time.

I wrote four new plays, expanded a shorter work into a longer one-act, and did extensive revisions to several others.

I got to see two of my plays live on stage. A half a dozen other works were used in staged readings and Zoom broadcasts, including readings that originated from Dallas, Texas, and London, England.

I had a chance to perform a dream role when I was cast as Leonard in Circle Players' production of "Seminar." Then a few weeks later, I landed a plum role in Playhouse 22's production of "Harvey," currently on hiatus, but ready to get started again once this virus gets under control.

I was re-elected to another term on the local School Board just in time to serve as Vice President in the most challenging and dynamic year in the history of the district.

I saw one son graduate from Rutgers and another one get accepted in NYU's graduate school for journalism.

When my oncologist suggested we slow down treatments because of the COVID-19 risk, I emphatically told him "no."

I watched Lisa once again build a business, absorb the blow of the COVID shutdown, and just keep going with online and outdoor classes, sometimes in complete renegade fashion.

My own consulting business grew. I'm busier than ever.

I became a grand-uncle when my niece gave birth to her new son, Colby. He was barely over one pound when he was born, but has thrived ever since, and is now home with his parents.

Over the past year, even the mundane (like eating my first Hydrox cookie in a decade, riding my new bike to the bagel shop, or being greeted by the wagging tail of my dog) canceled out the occasional discomforts. I never stop thinking about how lucky I have been. And I'm blessed to have so many people pulling for me. I can't thank everyone enough.

What will the next year bring? Frankly, I have no idea. What I do know is that the future is now. So I need to get back to teaching myself how to play the ukulele (thanks for the inspiration, Grace!). Fittingly, I am starting to learn a pretty passable version of "Old Man."

SEPTEMBER 7, 2020

I feel a sense of revenge this summer since the mosquitos are drinking chemo-infused blood.

In the meantime, cancer be damned. I just received two New Jersey Association of Community Theater nominations for both acting and writing (And First Avenue Theater's production of "Pets and Their Humans" picked up two more nominations). Amazed. Honored. Thankful.

The pending start of the Jewish high holidays (you know the one in which God writes in the Book of Life your fate for the coming year? Yeah, that one) got me thinking again of where I am, and more importantly where I'm going. Here I am with Addy, who kindly administered my latest cancer scan (she complemented me for being her "happiest" patient of the day). Keep in mind that I am feeling pretty good these days, probably better than I have in the last few years (as I say, I'm as healthy as a horse, if the horse had cancer), so I had high hopes we would see even further erosion of my tumor. Instead, it seems my tumor has the mentality of a NYC tenant lucky enough to being living in a rent controlled apartment and isn't interested in leaving. My doctor told me it was highly unlikely for chemo alone to wipe out a pancreatic tumor, so I have to admit I am fortunate that it remains unchanged in size and that my liver has been in remission now for six months. My good fortune doesn't negate my natural competitiveness. I still want to get rid of the little sucker.

Currently, my body is a police state. The chemo police have all the cells on lockdown. In the general scheme of things, that's a good thing. My doctor cheerfully pointed out that 80% of his patients are usually off chemo in a year. It was easier for him not to explain why those other patients don't need chemo anymore.

I am fortunate that my body tolerates chemo well. It's not a fun drug. It's not fun to carry a bag of the stuff for two days attached to a port in your chest. You manage the nausea and the exhaustion the best you can. Chemo takes away a few days every month, but it has also given me back more days than were expected when we started this treatment more than a year ago.

The trade-off is worth it. Unfortunately, for the moment, we have no idea how long this chemical partnership will last.

Over the past year, people touched with cancer have asked me for advice. I continue to emphasize that you need to focus your energies on the things you can control. By extension, you accept those things you can't. I can't tell my chemo what to do. I can't eliminate the uncertainty of a life now measured every two months by CAT scans. I can't tell you if I will ever be cured, or even what the means.

When I was younger, I always worried about growing old. Now that I'm on the cusp of being old, I'm learning it really isn't that bad. I still wake up every day wondering what will be new and unexpected. Learning to be old is almost as challenging as learning to live with cancer.

Which brings us back to the Book of Life. Jews are asked not to be perfect. Just be the perfect version of yourself. Rabbi Zusya once said, "In the world to come, they will not ask me 'Why were you not Moses? They will ask me, "Why were you not Zusya?"

As long as the chemo continue to work, I have an obligation to continue to live, to learn, to grow. It is an obligation we all share.

Shanah tovah.

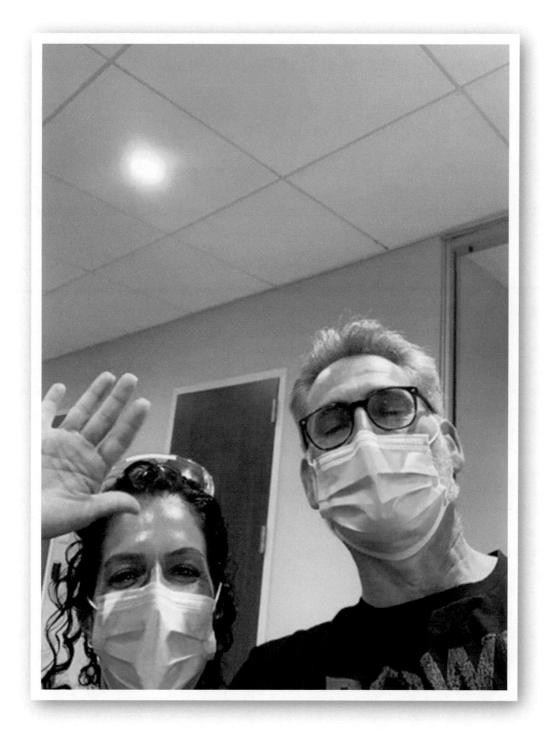

OCTOBER 3, 2020

Shortly after I learned about my cancer diagnosis, I made a vow that no matter what happened, I was going to see the completion of the Holmdel 2020 project. Thirty one chemo treatments later, I was honored to be allowed to say a few words at this week's ribbon cutting ceremony in front of the new entrance of the Holmdel High School. This is what I said:

The other day I was listening to an old Doors album called "Strange Days," and frankly Jim Morrison could have been singing about today. Wildfires and killer hurricanes. Political division and urban unrest. A slumping economy and a resilient pandemic. And that was just in August.

Today, the circumstances are a little brighter. We gather to affirm the power of community—the ability to put aside our differences and focus our energies instead on the common good. We celebrate new classrooms, new academic and artistic programs, new athletic fields, and new systems to protect the safety and well-being of our students and our staff.

In sum, you could say Oscar Wilde was at least half right when he said you can never be overdressed or overeducated.

Today we also affirm that our most precious resource is our children. When you look around, you see a laboratory for hope and optimism, allowing our children to reach their full potential and to develop the confidence to address the problems that elude us today and the problems we can't even anticipate tomorrow.

Benjamin Franklin once said that "an investment in knowledge always pays the best interest." What we have done here is to put our investment in our children, and in doing so, prepare them for their own "strange days" ahead. Only then, will they be able to, in the words of Jim Morrison, "break on through to the other side."

——

I'm so lucky to live in a community that has its priorities straight when it comes to public education. It's been a honor to serve on the Board of Education and to work with so many of my Board colleagues, past and present, to make truly great things happen.

More to come!

OCTOBER 4, 2020

Three weeks after I began my chemo treatments, I received a message from a local entertainer, <u>Larry Cutrone</u>, who knew me from my playwriting. It strikes me that "local" is too limiting a description. Larry was a man who seemed to be everywhere, a singer, producer, and writer with boundless, positive energy. He was also surviving his own bout with cancer, defying the odds and spitting into the wind.

He opened up about his own struggle with me and encouraged me to do the same. Our conversations were frank, loving, and inspirational. We chose to be memorable patients at our respective clinics. Larry, in particular, would bring along his ukulele and hold impromptu concerts. Staff at MSK nicknamed me the "happy" patient. Our wager with God was simple—as long as we woke up that morning, we would seize the day and squeeze as much out of it as we could.

Larry planned to produce a one act festival at the Darress Theatre in Boonton in June that would feature works we had both written, but when the coronavirus struck, that effort, like so many theatrical endeavors, was put on hold. Larry never lost his appreciation that his treatment had given him two more years when his original diagnosis gave him only two months. His spirit was strong, but in our most recent conversations, I could tell that Larry was beginning to wear down. I had planned to call him on Saturday, but I was too late. He quietly passed during the night.

I would say rest in peace, Larry, but I suspect he'll be too busy for that. The nightclub in heaven has a new headliner tonight, armed with a smile, a joke and plenty of songs to share.

More to come!

OCTOBER 30, 2020

Over the summer I read "The Emperor of All Maladies," a book about the history of cancer, written by Siddhartha Mukherjee, an oncologist. Siddhartha called his work a biography, and it's easy to see why. Cancer isn't a disease. It's a rebellion. A group of rogue cells rewire your DNA, and then they try to take over. Of course, if they win, everyone loses.

After 14 months of chemo, a ragtag group of malignant rebels are making a last stand inside a pancreatic citadel about a centimeter in size. My liver has been cancer-free for roughly ten months, so my oncologist thought the time was right to shift tactics.

On Thursday, I talked with two impossibly young cancer specialists who seemed only a few years removed from blasting away video game "bosses" between beers at a frat house. Now they have bigger gun at their disposal—targeted blasts of radiation designed to kill the remaining tumor. They liked to toss around confusing new words that may prove handy in a round of Scrabble, like ablative.

These guys were serious.

The approach calls for daily doses of radiation over a three-week period. No one has indicated yet if I will end up glowing in the dark.

One of the doctors made a curious remark during our discussion. He said I have "earned" this treatment, because my body reacted so well to my chemo. I had to smile because that what my knees said, too.

Some background. Over the last few weeks, I have been receiving side treatments from a local Reiki healer. Kim is a lovely woman with very warm hands and a curious ability to talk to my knees. I have learned that my knees nag a lot. They complain to Kim if I haven't eaten enough celery or they tell her that I should avoid bananas.

During my most recent treatment, my knees assured her that my body is working hard to fight back. So true. And now it's getting rewarded with a brand-new weapon to do so.

NOVEMBER 12, 2020

Over the last year and a half, I have visited Memorial Sloan Kettering every two weeks to receive my dose of chemotherapy. I'm fortunate that it hasn't been a lonely journey, and so many of you have faithfully followed my observations along the way. For that, I will always be grateful.

My first visit is depicted below. The most recent session took place last weekend. Today, I learned that it might be my last. I had been conditioned to believe that stopping chemotherapy would be an end-stage event. Now I'm being asked to reconsider what the end really means. While I still have a tumor in my pancreas, the metastatic cancer has been in remission for over ten months. We are talking about something potentially miraculous--a stage four diagnosis in reverse.

In the meantime, a group of hotshot radiation oncologists plan to use my body as a video game in December. A member of the medical team told me that past outcomes of MSK's radiation treatment are similar to surgery, in the sense that it is designed to eliminate the cancer. He quickly noted I'm an unusual case. He meant that in a good way.

Last Friday, a doctor performed an endoscopy to place slivers of gold in my pancreas to provide the "ray gun" with a target. The ultrasound gave him the first real look at my pancreas since my treatment began. He said beyond the site of the tumor (which he emphasized was incredibly small) the rest of the organ looked like it never had cancer in the first place.

This all feels a little surreal. I think about all the strange coincidences that have led me to this point in time, such as how I managed to find myself living only 11 minutes from one of only two hospitals in the entire United States that offer the cutting edge radiation procedure I will receive.

"Life, if well lived, is long enough," said the Roman philosopher Seneca. We all have limited time. Cancer simply makes that truism more vivid. I don't see myself closer to a cure. I see myself having an opportunity to accomplish a few more things before the window closes shut. And I feel fortunate that God has made me more aware of the urgency that we should all keep in the back of our minds.

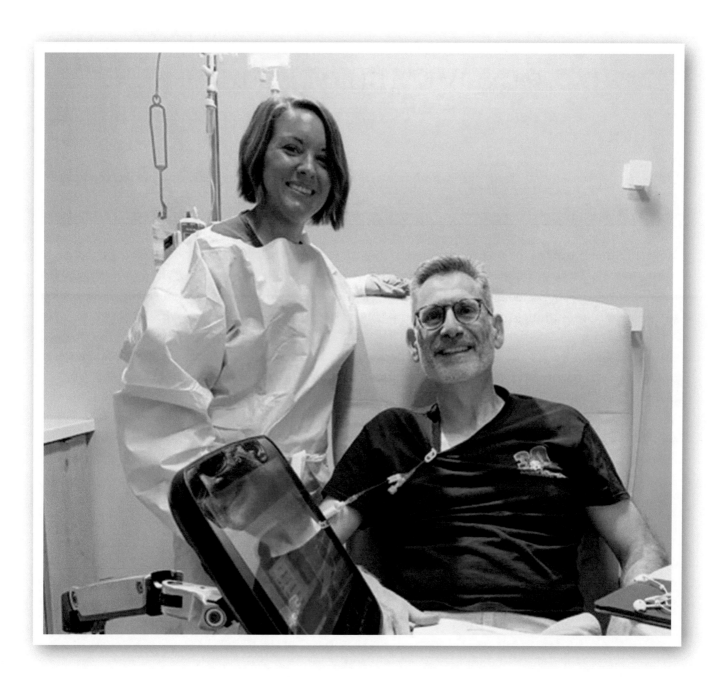

NOVEMBER 12, 2020

Today, three women tied up my arms, took off my shirt, put tattoos on my body and tickled my belly.

Bondage? Nope just preparation for my upcoming radiation treatments. Sorry to get you all excited.

It's ironic that purple is the color associated with pancreatic cancer, because politically, I see myself as purple as well. My town is filled with Republicans and run by Republicans. I work with Republicans all the time, I have been supported by Republicans (and vice versa), and I have worked closely with Republicans to tackle key community issues. My watchword is "assume positive intent."

But I can't ignore what my eyes tell me. The national Republican Party is executing a systematic attempt to steal the presidential election. This is not about Trump. This about his Orwellian enablers who are trying to undermine our democratic traditions. They are doing a nice job of packaging their nefarious activities under the guise of "fairness" and "ensuring every vote is counted" while they actively seek to do the exact opposite. Their recent efforts to reach out to influence local elections boards and prevent the certification of results is truly scary. People from both parties need to stand up and make it clear that what is going on is wrong

DECEMBER 6, 2020

Over the last week, I have gotten a new appreciation for TV dinners. Not as a culinary delight, but what they must be going through when you pop them into a microwave. Radiation is painless, so it is tough to really sense what's going on under your skin as technicians beam lethal doses to zap your tumor. The margin of error is small. I'm reminded regularly that there is this piece of small intestine nearby that doesn't really appreciate the sudden burst of sunshine. My radiation oncologist assures me everything is fine. I'm not unnerved by the fact that he has a tendency of having "walking" Facetime calls.

Radiation has also introduced a new type of nausea. I suppose many of you must think there is only one type of nausea--that queasy feeling that forces you to pray to the porcelain goddess throughout the night. Chemo introduced me to what I would call low-grade nausea, a multi-day experience in which you know its there, but you got to eat anyway, because if you don't, you die. BTW, the chemo also gives you a harbinger of what COVID does to your sense of taste. Chemo makes everything taste weird. Having a mother who taught be to eat everything off my plate trained me well to meet the challenges of this chemo-induced nausea.

Radiation nausea is a different world. It's like a knife attack. I can't eat before radiation, so I have to eat afterwards, because I can't take my new chemo pills on an empty stomach. Radiation nausea, anti-nausea meds, and chemo pills are old friends from their beer hall days, and they love to gang up on you. The chemo won't let you sleep, the anti-nausea meds sap out your energy, and the radiation keeps reminding you of the food still gurgling in your stomach. 33 chemo treatments taught me how to keep the vomit reflex under control, but it ain't easy.

Fortunately, they give me a weekend break. And I still got my hair. And my Reiki healer says that my knees still say positive things to her.

My primary oncologist (who could frankly make a good department store Santa) reiterated as long as they can't find any cancer outside of the pancreas, there is no reason to continue chemo treatments. Two more weeks of radiation, and I'm done. At least unless we see what the next cancer scan shows.

The radiation teams are also getting a first hand look at the strategy I used with the chemo nurses. When my father started to realize that he was suffering from dementia, he took a courageous and remarkable course of action. He made fun of everything, including himself. I thought that might be a good approach for addressing the absolute absurdity of all of this. Why take cancer seriously? Why not dance and sing and act silly? When am I going to get another chance? My reputation as this energetic crazy man who keeps throwing off stupid jokes is spreading within the radiation unit. As the plaque that sat on the desk of an old boss used to say, "Never be boring."

Or as my good friend <u>Krissy Fless</u> would say, "f@ck cancer."

DECEMBER 13, 2020

Diwali, Hanukkah, Kwanzaa and Christmas are holidays that celebrate light, which is no surprise given that November and December are among the darkest months of the year. There is a driving human need to cast light into the darkness, either physically or metaphorically. I'm going to offer some thoughts on the latter.

This week, I will complete my last five days of radiation treatment (My radiation oncologist and I joked last week that each photon shot is like lighting a candle in my internal menorah). Then I'm done. Fourteen months of chemo and I'm still standing. My oncologist told me last week there is no reason to continue to give me chemo if he can't find any cancer. In about eight weeks, we will learn if the radiation eradicated the final tumor, and if so, my life going forward will be measured by periodic scans.

I'm very lucky to be where I am right now. I will get to enjoy the holidays I never expected to see. A dark future pierced by the lights all around me. But these lights are also there to remind me that there are plenty of people who have not been so lucky. Certainly, Covid has taken quite a toll in the United States--over 300,000 deaths expected by the end of 2020. At the same time, as dramatic as that figure is, it still represents only half the number of people who will die from cancer this year. And there is no magic vaccine available to protect those who will be diagnosed with this disease in 2021.

This brings us back to the lights. Francis Bacon once wrote, "In order for the light to shine so brightly, the darkness must be present." Darkness serves as a tableau to make those memories we cherish brighter still. We can view the lights of the holidays as a way to replicate the lights once cast off by a loved one. The holidays become a time to celebrate those no longer with us physically, but still alive and vibrant within our minds. Our ability to remember is the true miracle of the season.

Seasons greetings.
May your own holidays be merry and bright.

FEBRUARY 28, 2021

Rich is a greeter. It's always a competition to see which of us is going to have the bigger smile when I come by the MSK clinic in Middletown for a visit (underneath the mask, of course). Frankly, the smile was little more forced than usual when I came by to discuss my latest scan in February. After 18 months of chemo and a radiation holocaust in my pancreas, we are sort of back to where we started as my cancer returned to my liver. And that's when I learned the latest results are actually a good thing. Let me explain.

Shortly after I was diagnosed with cancer, I signed some papers that allowed Memorial Sloan Kettering to do a genetic scan of my body. That information gets thrown in a database accessed by medical investigators conducting clinical trials.

Turns out that I have something called a mutated RET proto-oncogene which triggers the growth of my pancreatic cancer. More importantly, the FDA approved last year a drug that inhibits RET in lung and thyroid cancer with pretty dramatic results. Researchers want to see if they can have similar success with other cancers (there are some early indications that it does work with cancers that originate from the pancreas).

The basic idea around the study is to determine the optimal dosage for the drug, which is called Selpercatinib. I understand the Disney people originally planned to use that name for a song in "Mary Poppins," but "Supercalifragilisticexpialidocious" won out in the end.

Suddenly, I'm pretty popular, as in the Sally Field "you like me" realm of popular. Paperwork asking me to join this new clinical trial arrived only hours after my oncologist shared his reading of my latest scan. I've heard they might entice me with a new toaster oven. Even the pills are free.

My new best buddy is Dr. Drilon, who has been leading clinical trials around this drug for years. With a name like that you might expect him to a dentist or a power tool manufacturer. Seems like a good guy.

Of course, in the Catch 22 world of modern medicine, you can't take a drug designed to knock out your cancer unless they can find cancer to knock out. So in a weird way, chemo's failure to finish the job allows me to take what might end up being a better drug anyway.

The trial requires me to head up to New York City weekly so the researchers can closely monitor me. But I also understand that if I can make it there, I can make it anywhere.

It's up to you New York.

APRIL 10, 2021

This March was one of those months that you want to grind up, stuff into a trash bag, piss all over it, cover it in lighter fluid and watch it joyfully go up in flames.

Or maybe it would best to describe my March as a car wreck, like my beautiful Volvo, hit on Route 34 on a clear night, while going at the speed limit of around 45 miles an hour, by a "distracted" driver going so fast that he literally sheared off my right back wheel. I still don't understand how I didn't lose control of the car or that it didn't tip over. Once again, another testimonial for Volvo safety. But maybe not their logistics. The repair shop is still waiting for parts to arrive from Sweden.

March was also the month I started a new clinical trial. Truthfully, there was very little "new" about this drug. It had already been FDA approved for two other cancers, where the response rate had been excellent and sustainable. It matched the genetic makeup of my cancer and was designed to target the gene that was generating my cancer cells and turn it off. A true miracle drug. The MSK clinical team had been eagerly following my case. They had wanted me for months. Their lead researcher had been working with hundreds of patients for over three years. I mean, what could go wrong?

Hold that thought.

The trial required me to go to NYC at the start. The facility on the city's east side had the quiet buzz of efficiency. Patient people processing thousands of patients. Unsuspecting the whirlwind just about to burst through those elevator doors, a memorable presence ready to give a positive poke to everyone everywhere. No one was safe.

As I munched my sandwich in the sixth floor cafeteria, a stranger turned to me and said I'm the most positive person he has ever met. I slowly nodded. Mom taught me never to talk with my mouth full.

The clinical trial people were putty in my hands. I quickly put the receptionists in tears as I kept lobbing jokes like hand grenades. The nurses were peppering me with questions, a mere formality, but it was tough to stay serious when they earnestly told me that during the trial, I am absolutely forbidden to go around impregnating women. I responded that I would only focus my attentions on menopausal ones.

During the first few weeks of the trial, I developed a nagging, dry cough, and a series of low fevers. COVID was ruled out, X-rays show clear lungs, but my energy was slowly leaking out like a balloon with a small hole. I begged the team to give me anti-biotics (a request eventually granted a week later which knocked out the cough in two days as I expected), but the medical folks were distracted by disturbing liver numbers. I was told to stop taking the drug at the end of March, and when I appeared at my next clinical visit on April 6, I found myself unexpectedly whisked into the hospital for tests and monitoring.

They needed to figure out what was wrong with my liver and why. No one could say how long they thought I would have to stay. With literally the clothes on my back and a business computer without a charger, I had my sons put together a CARE package and my amazing friend, Vicky Flynn delivered it to the NYC (she even had a spare computer charger).

Suddenly I had become a NASA project with three separate medical teams "working the problem." A young man with the air of counterculture waited to transport me to my ultrasound. We started to talk about music. The cough was now gone thanks to modern medicine, so there I was rolling down a hallway, belting out "Gold Dust Woman" while we wheeled briskly into the room. A version of "Fly Me to the Moon" got the tech folks asking for encores as the ultrasound technician with the foreign accent smiled and did her job. I asked her how the liver looked. "Fine," she said. "Just bigger."

In sum, the cancer drug was beating up the liver, and it was inflamed. I was put immediately on heavy doses of steroids. The head of the liver team, a young guy with a penchant for sweatshirts who seem ready to head off to the next college kegger was keeping his cards close to his chest. I could be there for two days or eleven. It depended upon how quickly my liver bounced back. But at least there were no obstructions and no need for medical procedures.

My nurses like Ashley were widely competent. Ashley's colleague, Debra, who filled in on Ashley's day off, has a child in medical school. She had this clocklike precision around everything she did. On the first night I suddenly woke up at one in the morning to find two nurses feverishly covering me with icepacks to bring down one of my fevers, which was covering me with sweat.

Thursday didn't show too much movement, but on Friday morning, the oncological team burst in at 8 a.m. with that level of enthusiasm that should come with a soundtrack. Tapping on cell phones and smiling broadly, they told me the liver had bounced back dramatically, and that after that day's afternoon treatment I could go home. My liver, the recipient of years of "almost" clean living, was once again imitating Gumby, as it has throughout my treatment.

Lots of thanks to staff, a walk about the floor singing loudly, and then I'm in the back of a Lincoln limo, tired and contemplative. Of course, the house was in slight disarray when I came home, and I spend the early hours cleaning the bathroom where we keep the kitty litter boxes.

I had it keep it contained so well, but as I told the social worker who had stopped by earlier in the day, the emotions were going to come out eventually. I had a few things to say to God. In the darkness of my garage, I let him have it. Through angry tears and a raspy voice, I told him in no uncertain terms that I wasn't quitting. I told he was going to have try a lot harder if he wanted me to come upstairs. I told him I wasn't done. I don't know why, but deep in my heart I knew that.

Later in a quieter moment, God and I agreed to keep talking. Or at least I did. Negotiations are never over.

APRIL 23, 2021

Foie Gras is one of those interesting examples in which human ingenuity and cruelty intersect. Just imagine feeding a duck or goose an excessive amount of food to make sure their livers swell to ten times their normal volume to produce a culinary delicacy. I'm sure it's tasty. The recipe dates back to the ancient Egyptians.

Been thinking about Foie Gras lately because my own sad and swollen liver has the medical team at MSK stumped. Today, we increase the steroids by 50% and we are scrambling to set up more medical tests to get to the bottom of the problem. Without a happy liver, we can't proceed with the clinical trial, which has produced some good early returns.

Frustrated? Sure. Imagine being tied to a chair in the desert with a glass of water just out of arm's reach. But as I was reminded the other day, I am being treated by one of the top hospitals in the world. And the doctors have kept me going almost 22 months after the cancer was first discovered, which is pretty remarkable. I just need a little more positive energy headed my way. Telling my liver that if he doesn't get with the program that it might end up on a plate with Fava beans and a nice Chianti doesn't seem to be working.

APRIL 27, 2021

The question was simple. The tone was a little off. "Did you read the scan report?" asked Madeline, one of the nurse practitioners on my MSK medical team. Throughout the clinical trial, the first adjectives that come to mind when I think about Madeline is serious, business-like, and prepared. Befuddled was something all together new.

Of course, I had the report. It had arrived in my MSK email box roughly an hour after I received a series of CAT scans and MRIs on Friday. My cranky liver had prevented me from getting any anti-cancer treatment for almost a month. The last thing I wanted to do was look at my scan report.

"No," I said. "I thought I would wait until I heard your conclusions."

I lied. I was just too scared to look at it.

A pause. A long incredulous pause.

"No new growth," she said. "The cancer stayed the same."

Actually, that wasn't completely accurate. The scan also showed the spot in my pancreas itself had shrunk, potential evidence that all that radiation back in December did the trick. And the Monday blood work showed the liver enzyme count was dropping.

A little early to declare victory. Liver still has to heal. And we still need to find the right dose of my current drug. The road ahead could have some more bumps, but I'm blessed to have a pathway in the first place.

Over the last 22 months, I have been humbled by the prayers, the well wishes, and the relentless tide of positive thoughts.

And they are apparently working.

Thank you.

APRIL 30, 2021

Just finished the first draft for a radio play for my English friends. In the process, I learned inadvertently that you can write pretty emotional stuff when you have been on steroids for three weeks.

Lesson one on how to charm nurses. During check in for my liver biopsy in NYC yesterday, one of the nurses asked if I have fallen recently. Too easy. I quickly responded, "Besides falling in love with you?" Liver enzymes levels continue to move in the right direction. Overall, feel good. Hopefully more progress next week.

JUNE 5, 2021

The MSK lobby in Monmouth was pretty empty when I stopped by for my scan last week. So I chatted a bit with the receptionist.

"Not too many people here, huh?" I asked.

"Yeah," he said. "It's practically dead in here."

Always love a good Freudian slip.

The clinical trial is over. My liver didn't want to cooperate, partly because some of the cancer wanted a water view, and settled near a bile duct. Those pesky enyzme numbers weren't going to go down on their own, so on the Saturday of Memorial Weekend I returned to chemo treatments.

In general, the new combination promises to be a little milder on the constitution, and I don't have to carry around a chemo pack for two days. There is a better chance I lose my hair, but it might simple thin, rather than fall out (one nurse pointed out if you got thick hair already, you probably will be safe. We'll see.)

The most important thing is that I have options, and if the chemo steadies the ship, we just wait until the next treatment comes along. The scan didn't show any growth in the pancreas itself, so maybe the radiation holocaust worked there.

About that "death" line? Well, I'm a little too busy to think about end state right now. On Saturday, one of the first plays I wrote after my diagnosis will be featured at the Middletown Arts Center's Festival of One Act plays--"Big in Texas." One of my better heartfelt works. The staged readings begins at 7 pm. Be good to support local theater, or at the bare minimum, just see theater again done live and in person.

Equally exciting is the fact that Playhouse 22 will go ahead with Harvey this fall, so if I hang in there (hair or no hair), I'll at least get a chance to act again on a stage. And literally minutes after I got that confirmation, the Villagers folks emailed that "In Danger of Falling in Love" is back on their schedule for next season, after being cancelled because of COVID. One of my plays gets a radio reading out of Chattanooga later this month, and I drafted two more plays over the last few weeks for two other companies.

At some point, the treatment was going to hit a snag. The key is to get back on the horse. And like I say to everyone, I'm as healthy as a horse. As long as the horse has cancer.

JUNE 12 AND 14, 2021

I'm not what you would call a heavy drinker by any means, but it is nice to be able to open up a cold beer from time to time or even a glass of scotch or rum on ice. Unfortunately, alcohol and cancer in your liver doesn't make a good combination, and I have been abstinent since February. I never realized how much I would miss it, or how alcohol plays such a major role in social gatherings. I have a renewed respect for those friends of mine who are recovering alcoholics who have managed to go for years fighting this urge. In the meantime, pass me that ginger ale, please.

I guess it's always a matter of perspective. When I went back on chemo three weeks ago, I didn't worry so much about the nausea or the exhaustion. I could always hide that. My main fear was losing my hair, so I quickly scheduled a picture shoot with a local photographer just in case. My favorite is my new profile photo (thanks for the nice comments).

Apparently, my timing was good, because beginning today, I started shedding like a cat. I guess I'll know in a few days if my thick hair will just get thinner or become history.

Sigh. Obviously, I understand the alternative isn't better, but I'll be honest. This ain't going to be easy for me. Wish me luck.

JULY 10, 2021

Spending the weekend in New York City in a lovely room overlooking the city's east side. Too bad it's a hospital room here at MSK. I did manage to charm the staff when I arrived on Thursday night with my usual routine of singing, dancing and semi-comical jokes. As a result, those on duty in the urgent care center pulled strings and placed me on the elegant 19th floor, a ritzy section of the hospital with single rooms usually reserved for VIPs. But then if I beat pancreatic cancer, I might be the biggest VIP of them all.

My latest NYC adventure began when they did my blood work prior to my latest chemo round. My liver numbers looked very bad, suggesting that one of my tumors was blocking a bile duct and later confirmed by my CAT scan. I'm scheduled for an endoscopic procedure on Monday to address it.

Initially, they wouldn't let me eat, just in case the procedure took place on Friday. I pointed out I'm only supposed to celebrate Yom Kippur once a year.

So I'm stuck in a hospital bed this weekend, because if I leave, I lose my place in line (Emergencies go first. The fact we are trying to avoid an emergency is irrelevant). The nurses are all sweet and pretty and naturally they are giving me (wait for it) the VIP treatment.

Doctors do stop by from time to time. One even came by at 3 a.m. I did manage to get one to let me get a peek at my scan results, which showed the largest liver tumor was shrinking at the same rate my pancreatic tumor shrank during the first round of chemo two years ago.

With those results in mind, I was a little amused when one doctor confidently told me today that the goal of a second round of chemo (that describes what I'm going through right now) is to just stop the cancer from growing. Maybe, I thought, he should aim higher.

AUGUST 14, 2021

The question is not how to get cured, but how to live."

--Joseph Conrad, Lord Jim

There is a fogginess that has settled over me, a drifting exhaustion that makes it difficult to do the things I wouldn't think twice about. It settled in after my latest round of chemo and it has proven relentless. Almost like the Elvis Costello's song, I have sunk into the Blue Chair, stuck and immobile.

Probably the most literate excuse you have ever read why I haven't been responsive to all those FB IMs, texts and phone messages.

After over 40 chemo treatments in roughly two years (not to mention putting stents to keep a liver duct open), one would have to expect the body to start to complain. And the Conrad quote continues to sum up my overall strategy. Don't take good days for granted. And even in the bad days, try to squeeze out something positive. For example, the latest photo was taken at the gym one day after my last chemo injection. And I did manage to walk a mile today (with feet numbed by neuropathy).

Doing my due diligence, too. Stopped by a funeral home the other day just to get a better idea what a "funeral" entails with a young manager doing his best to project the right amount of cheerfulness and somber respect. About fourteen minutes into our conversation, he stopped and took a close look at me. "You know," he said, with a head shake for additional emphasis, "you are the calmest person I have met."

Well, maybe it helps when you know that the traditional Jewish pine coffin only costs about $400.

The game plan is now a matter of endurance. Stick with a dose of chemo that will make the remaining cancer melt away like units of the Afghan regular army (or for those with long enough memories, the

ARVN in 1975). Eat through the nausea. Get out of the Blue Chair. Then hopefully in a few months, we reach a point when a more benign solution is available to keep everything in check.

Friends are important now. If the responses are slower or my voice sounds softer, just consider it a phase, not an end state. There are still enough warm days out there to spend a few minutes on my patio with Gatorade. "Facing it, always facing it, that's the way to get through", wrote Conrad. " Face it"

SEPTEMBER 11, 2021

Early on, I reached the conclusion that the best approach for addressing my cancer challenge was to try to stay even keel. It hasn't been easy, especially in 2021, which has been a roller coaster ride built around failed clinical trials, tumors taking pleasure cruises through my liver lobes, and fluid backups that would make you think I had a personal visit from Hurricane Ida. I spent most of August zombie-like—bloating, nausea, weight loss, and a general malaise which made it impossible to do the simplest things.

The Thursday before Labor Day weekend was the nadir. My scan showed excessive flooding on my liver, bilirubin numbers too high to tolerate chemo, and my cancer still growing. Even a local funeral director was frightened by my appearance, and this is a guy whose business is built around dead people.

My doctor sent me back to the hospital in NYC where I was a greeted by a French doctor with a sexy, unintelligible accent. I think he said that we needed to put in a drain. Or he might have been commenting about oranges in Spain. Either way I nodded my head and told him to do what he must. He and his team drained two liters of fluid from my liver and put in an active drain in my right side which continues to collect bile on an ongoing basis in a plastic bag. Every day, I feel a little bit better, and while there is still more improvement to make, my oncologist did say the bilirubin numbers are now low enough to allow him to restart chemo, using a version of the original combination that I tolerated well.

Balloons? Confetti? No yet. It isn't easy, but I need to keep my perspective on the bigger picture.

Learn to roll with change and stay focused on the final prize. "Choose to be optimistic," said the Dalai Lama. "It feels better."

OCTOBER 29, 2021

I watched the other day a video op-ed about the positives around quitting. Narrated by the New York Times' Lindsay Crouse, her primary message was don't be a "martyr to grit." In fact, giving up seems to be a popular subject these days in our pandemic-tinged world, and people everywhere are giving themselves permission to quit things they no longer like doing, such as their careers.

Quitting is easy, and life is hard. Or as Nintendo is kind to remind us, "Are you sure you want to quit? All unsaved progress will be lost."

Those closest to me know that the last few months have been brutal. When bile leaks out of your liver, forms a pool in your abdominal cavity and begins to press against your organs, you got a problem. It took six weeks to drain mine, and two weeks ago, my collection bag was finally removed. The primary question was how we keep it from returning.

So, there I was lying on a hospital gurney about to be wheeled into surgery to put another stent in a liver duct, when I met Dr. Getrajdman, a veteran surgeon who had been doing this sorta thing for about 30 years. He was about to deliver the fifth official explanation of the potential outcome of the procedure I was about to experience (without the indecipherable French accent of his predecessor). The good news was it looked like the drain was working. The bad news was half my liver was failing, and I risked killing that portion of it if I didn't take corrective action.

He assured me that I could get along nicely with half a liver. Somehow, I suspect Hannibal Lector used to say the same thing.

Unfortunately, the corrective action wasn't so simple. With two stints already in place, it would be difficult to add a third one. The doctor said although he knew his share of "tricks," there was only a 50-50 chance he could pull it off. The alternative was a permanent tube and a bag tied to my leg. I had to make choice— take the risk or lose half my liver.

It was a fool's choice. I probably had the best stent man in the hospital in my corner, and he would view it as a personal defeat if he had to put in a "tube and bag." My biggest concern was that he knew I wanted to be a centerfielder for the Red Sox when I grew up while his childhood aspiration was to play shortstop for the Yankees.

I told him to save my liver.

When the fog of the anesthesia lifted, I was glad to notice a tube wasn't sticking out of my chest. So glad in fact that I celebrated an hour later by vomiting (my reaction to the anesthesia encouraged me to vomit about a half a dozen times for the rest of the day and throughout the night). Later that evening, a relieved Dr. Getrajdman visited me, sharing the same satisfied look worn by the pilot who shot down the Red Baron. He told me it was only the fourth time in 30 years of surgery that he pulled off putting in a third stint. So much for 50-50 odds. At least he had a new triumphant story to share at upcoming cocktail parties on Long Island.

I had to stay in the hospital longer than planned because I had fever spikes after the surgery, and they needed to make sure I didn't have an infection. Fortunately, I didn't, but it gave the medical people an excuse to scan the region to make sure the new stent worked. The last doctor to see me said it would be okay to go home even though my bilirubin numbers (which measure the overall health of my liver) were still high. I asked this doctor if they would go down soon, because high numbers could affect my ability to get chemo.

When he failed to give a straight answer (the official medical term is "hemming and hawing"), I decided to be the adult in the room and said my experience had been that it usually takes a little time for the liver to heal from the trauma of someone poking around in it. The doctor's response was a scholarly nod in agreement. And I was right. I learned on this Thursday before my latest chemo round that the numbers had dropped from the high threes to just a few decimal points above normal. The scan also gave my oncologist an opportunity to peek at my cancer. The new chemo seems to be keeping the cancer in check, and he described my overall status as "encouraging." Even my hair is growing back.

Maybe quitting works for some people. I don't have that option. "The future bears down upon each one of us with all the hazards of the unknown," wrote the Greek historian Plutarch "The only way out is through it."

DECEMBER 26, 2021

Christmas week marked my 29th month of treatment. Somehow it seemed fitting that the MSK nurses and I would celebrate my 46th round of chemo by playing Bell Biv DeVoe's song "Poison" on my iPhone.

A lot of people tell me that I'm looking good these days, which is promising since there are days in which it feels like my insides are more like the Portrait of Dorian Gray. The goal now is to pursue a new normal in which my cancer becomes chronic rather than fatal. At the same time, the overall uncertainty of my condition can make it difficult for some people. They worry needlessly about things, like maybe I need to slow down and not "overdo it." To me, that advice just becomes another way of saying I should retire to my bed and wait for the inevitable. Of course, I don't see that as an option.

Staying busy is synonymous to staying alive, and as you can tell by the way I use my walk, I'm a ladies man, no time to talk. I just want to be treated as someone operating above the earth, rather than below it.

When you face the prospect of the Long Goodbye, an additional challenge is nostalgia, which almost always leads to second guessing about the choices you made and the life you lived. I suspect I would do things differently if I had been given the chance, but then, I can't guarantee those choices would have led me down a better path.

In a perverse way, any disease can be seen as a gift of sorts, a reminder that our time is limited and that we need to take advantage of it. I plan to do new things in 2022 and stay as active as I can. I encourage you to join in the adventure (or at least do whatever you can to encourage me to get out of the house).

Happy New Year everyone.

JANUARY 9, 2022

The mantra of realtors everywhere is "location, location, location." You could say the same thing about cancer.

Last summer, a small but growing tumor was in the wrong place, blocking a liver duct and causing bile to back up into my abdominal cavity. A team of doctors huddled around my hospital bed, outlining a variety of surgical options. I offered one of my own. Won't the chemo eventually cause the tumor to shrink, solving the problem in the first place?

The senior doctor of the group offered a remarkably blunt response. "That never happens," he said.

I think I smiled a little bit when I heard that. I love a challenge. I was going to prove him wrong.

Last week's medical check-up and chemo treatment included a review of my latest CAT scan, the first since October. The body language of the medical team was good, so I suspected the results were going to be positive. While I was waiting for my turn to see my oncologist, he poked his head in the room and said, "The scan looks good. I think we'll give you chemo today." And then he disappeared just as quickly.

When we finally met, he said most of the tumors were the same, while two of them shrank.

"How much?" I asked.

This question threw him for a loop. He hadn't done the calculations. He gave an estimated range of 10 to 20 percent.

"Can I see the lab report?" I asked. He handed it to me. He confirmed that one of the shrinking tumors was located near my liver duct.

Math isn't my strong suit, but it seemed to make sense to compare the square area of the tumor then and now to get a sense of what sort of progress had been made. After the doctor's visit, I asked a nurse if that sounded right. She said she thought so. By the way, medical people have a habit of saying that a lot.

I ran the numbers, made an initial mistake of adding instead of multiplying, and then checked the numbers two more times. The surface area of the liver duct tumor had shrunk almost 50%, while the largest tumor on my liver shrunk by at least 40%.

Meanwhile the report said that the original tumor in my pancreas was "poorly defined" with signs of atrophy, suggesting the radiation treatment I received at the end of 2020 had turned that malignancy into scar tissue.

The next day, I was talking to one of the nurses to confirm the numbers, since there were typos in the two reports, and I wanted to make sure everything was aligned. During our conversation, I had to ask her if it was unusual to see results like these almost 30 months into treatment. She conceded that they were "rare." Even on the phone, you could tell she was smiling about that.

My advice? When it comes to medical prognosis, a little selected "skepticism" never hurts. And the prayers are working.

MARCH 17, 2022

After completing my 56th round of chemo, I headed to a local restaurant to take advantage of their annual St. Patrick's Day special (corned beef, boiled potatoes, cabbage, and soda bread for under $8. That's the type of bargain that would make my Dad proud). The computers were down, and the waitress asked with some embarrassment if I could wait for the check. Of course, I said. By that point, I was too fascinated watching the Saint Peters University game to leave the place. A small Jesuit school from Jersey City was about to humble Kentucky, which boasts the winningest program in the history of NCAA basketball. In contrast, St. Pete's NCAA Tournament record now stands at a lofty 1-3.

Watching an underdog triumph in overtime got me thinking. I'm also an underdog fighting in overtime against an opponent that rarely loses. God and medical science have put me here. And I'm not playing out the clock.

In fact, it's been a good week for underdogs. Last month, I got an email from the Director of Acquitions at Broadway Licensing, the owners of the Dramatists Play Service and one of the top theatrical licensing and play publishing services in the world. He read two of my plays, "Horseshoes" and "Pets (and Their Humans)," and he wanted worldwide licensing rights for them, which includes publications.

My conversations with him and his Acquistions Manger were helpful and professional. For two people who made their living out of drama, there was clearly none of it present during the negotiating process.

It's probably on the edge of irony that the last play I had planned to do before sickness forced me to the sidelines was "Harvey," a proud member of the DPS portfolio. On Tuesday, I signed a contract to join it.

How this all came about is probably so convoluted and miraculous I would be at loss at how to explain it, so I will default to something easier to fathom. Underdogs do win sometimes, just like St. Peters. After a long day at the office, God must kick back with a few beers and watch my little black comedy of a life with amusement. It must be too fascinating to cancel right now.

MARCH 23,2022

I have been reading lately Ron Chernow's remarkable biography of Ulysses S. Grant, one of the most misunderstood presidents in American history. In the final year of his life, Grant raced to complete his memoirs before he succumbed to throat cancer. He finished his final draft only days before his death. Mark Twain, a personal friend who knew a little something about writing, was astounded by the quality of work, especially considering the challenges Grant faced to complete it.

It may be a little early to determine where my finish line lies, but I do sense a similar challenge. When I started writing plays about eight years ago, I focused on the output, not the promotion. I have been extraordinarily lucky and blessed. I'm still amazed there are actors out there willing to take the time and energy to bring my words to life.

Tuesday night, six actors gathered around the table for the first read-through of my play, "In Danger of Falling in Love," which will debut on the weekends of May 13th and May 20th at the Villagers Theater in Somerset. Normally, I simply enjoy listening to the words, but the real joy tonight came from watching the genuine delight on the faces of the actors as they followed the story. This is really going to be good.

Just a little warning, fair readers. Expect a lot of nagging from me over the next few weeks to buy tickets.

"Everyone has his superstitions," Grant once said. "One of mine has always been when I started to go anywhere, or to do anything, never to turn back or to stop until the thing intended was accomplished."

A race has only one direction. When it ends is less important than how you finish.

APRIL 10, 2022

Spent Saturday sitting at the counter of the relentlessly busy Keyport Diner, eating a waffle smothered in fruit and recuperating from my first business trip in more than two years. The company planned "back to the office" celebrations, and I indicated to my boss that I would be willing to travel out to Colorado. I hadn't been in an office since COVID struck, and I missed the old business rhythms that comes from talking to colleagues face to face.

Of course, the entire idea made no sense at all. I was asking my body to tolerate a flight across two time zones only days after my 57th chemo treatment (I understand I now qualify for a lifetime supply of Heinz products). I was going to sit through two days of meetings, participate in a few after work activities (like dinner with members of the Comm team), and stay energetic and focused through the whole thing. Even in the best of health, I was tackling something that promised to a bit audacious.

But I also saw it as a test. How far could I push myself? Would I let my cancer dictate my actions or vice versa? In this context, I let my natural competitiveness take over.

The first two days of the trip were brutal. My intestinal system seemed to be in constant distress and the high altitude didn't help matters. My neuropathic feet kept reminding me that the office was practically a corporate Stairmaster. But my bow ties distracted people; they thought I looked good, and that helped disguise my symptoms pretty well.

By day three, I was starting to feel more normal, and by the last day, I was settled into my seat for the flight home, mission accomplished and an eager rendezvous with my bed only a few hours away.

And that's when things got really interesting.

I broke one of my cardinal rules by booking the last flight out. It was delayed, an early bad sign, but we also had on board a group of Rabbinical students, dutifully doing evening prayers.I assumed God would be listening. He wasn't.

Midway through the flight, we learned that Newark was closed by high winds, so naturally we were diverted to the "Windy City." It was chaos at O'Hare. Confused service representatives, struggling with computers that weren't working and muttering about their shifts coming to end. To lighten the mood, I started playing Eddie Floyd's, "Big Bird," on my iPhone. No one seemed amused.

It was time to pull out the "cancer card." I explained my medical condition to one representative who was conveniently standing next to a supervisor. I said my medicine was in my luggage, and I just wanted to get to a hotel and crash.They pulled me aside and put me in this "secret" room (it didn't even have a visible door) where they managed to resolve everything, including a connecting flight. About an hour later, I was in someplace called Schaumberg, talking to a hotel clerk who could have given lessons on being dour to Henry Winkler's character in the movie "Night Shift."

The following day was raw and rainy, spoiling plans to take a walking tour of Chicago and catch the Cubs in action at Wrigley. I went back to the airport, hoping to find an earlier flight. The best they could do was airdrop me into LaGuardia in the middle of the afternoon rush hour. The Uber driver couldn't speak English, leading to a lovely scenic tour of Staten Island on the way home, but by seven, I was comfortably lying in bed.

I was pleased that somehow my stamina held up, even late at night as I negotiated myself out of the mess in Chicago. Ultimately the winning factor once again was my persistent, New England stubborness. "Stubborn people get themselves in a lot of trouble," Anna Paquin once said. "But they also get things done."

APRIL !7, 2022

Passover isn't a great day for Egyptians. A megalomaniac leader, refusing another people's separate nationality, tries to crush them with overwhelming force, only to be surprised when his army gets wiped out by an unexpected intervention.

Sound familiar?

The Passover tale transcends religious beliefs and reflects the terrible circle of human interaction, in which there are always oppressors and people to be oppressed. Sometimes miracles happen, whether through the hand of God or a well-aimed Stinger missile.

You can internalize these battles, too. Recently a colleague of mine at work asked how I was doing and then stopped himself. "I bet you hate it when people ask you that all the time," he said.

Actually, no, especially when it is not perfunctory. The answer simply gets more complicated as my list of ailments grow. Neuropathy has left my hands clumsy and my feet numb. My liver remains grumpy. My bowels like to surprise me at the worst moments. I itch like crazy. I have mysterious brownouts reminiscent of overtaxed power grids during a California summer. Each day offers a new challenge, and they are usually not good ones.

Time may be on The Rolling Stones' side, but certainly not mine, but when you obsess about making every moment count, you find yourself paralyzed in achieving an impossible goal. I'm trying not to worry about the final cosmic impact of fixing a toilet. Or taking naps from time to time. When you try to create bucket lists, often you find your foot in one of them.

My rabbi kindly invited me to his house for Passover, and with my son in tow, I entered into a Sedar filled with noise, conversations, and boisterous reminders of life. I reminded him that on a night that we celebrate miracles, he decided to invite one into his house not named Elijah.

Passover and Easter represent moments of affirmation—one a triumph over evil, the other a triumph over death itself. It betrays the inherent optimism of humanity. Israeli professor Yuval Noah Harari expressed it this way, "You could never convince a monkey to give you a banana by promising him limitless bananas after death in monkey heaven." I don't worry how many bananas I have left to eat.

The best we can do is to try to enjoy each one. L'chiam.

APRIL 23, 2022

The volunteer rabbi from at MSK uttered the four words that every Jew dreads to hear—"They're coming for you." Of course, context is everything, and in this case the rabbi was seeking to be optimistic. After hours of fasting so that I could take general anesthesia safely, he was confident that my turn would come soon for my "procedure" to correct whatever was ailing my liver.

I was less hopeful. After endless itching, yellowing skin, and soaring bilirubin numbers, it wasn't safe for my jaundiced liver to tolerate chemo as well. My oncologist and I agreed to give it a weekend and see if the problem would correct itself. Instead the bilirubin levels doubled, and an early morning Lyft ride was in order to check into MSK's main campus in Manhattan.

MSK has been around since 1884, but I guess it still hasn't gotten a handle on scheduling, so my early morning arrival didn't automatically guarantee a time when I would receive my surgery.

Apparently, an email debate was happening behind the scenes as various doctors were offering competing strategies to treat me. One approach was to use an endoscopy to clean out my stents, but that ran a higher risk of infection. The other was a more direct approach to replace the stent outright. The first day I fasted for 16 hours only to be told at 4:30 p.m. that they weren't ready to see me. We were headed down the same path on Thursday, when a nurse practitioner stopped by to tell me who won—the doctor who put in my last stent back in the fall. He said he had taken a personal interest in my case.

On one hand, he was a talented surgeon filled with energy and confidence and a childhood desire to play shortstop for the Yankees (He was accepting of my similar dream to play centerfield for the Red Sox). On the other hand, this was the same guy who had told me at the time that I had a fifty-fifty chance of getting a permanent drain. Turned out that he wasn't even in the office. Another member of his team would do the work. He liked to look at his clipboard a lot with specific attention to the signature I just gave him consenting to the surgery. He explained he needed to replace one of the stents, the procedure his predecessor said was so challenging in the first place.

When I told him that I didn't want a drain, he smiled, reminded me he was a pretty good doctor, and that was not likely to happen. After he left, I confided in the nurse in the room that I was still a little nervous. "Oh, don't worry," she said. "He's been pretty competent today." Who can't be confident with a ringing endorsement like that?

Still it felt good to know that at least I was getting close to eating and drinking again, and I didn't mind entertaining the surgical nurses on the second floor with a few appropriate lyrics. They liked "Signed, sealed, delivered, I'm yours" as well as "Doctor, doctor, give me the news, I got a bad case of loving you."

Surgery went as planned; I woke up without a drain. Celebrated with a bowl of oatmeal and strawberries. And a big bag of homemade matzo dropped off by the rabbi. Apparently he was impressed by my upbeat mode. My bilirubin numbers remain high after the procedure, but that's not unusual. It can take days for the liver to get the message. For now, more of the same—cancer and hospital food. Not sure yet which should worry me more.

Sometimes things go bump in the night, and if you fail to follow Jim Morrison's advice ("keep your eyes on the road, your hands across the wheel"), those bumps might come to you.

A lesson learned while standing on Miller Avenue across from Costco in Hazlet. One day removed from returning from the hospital, I had nudged my Volvo wagon into a five year old BMW. Not a mark on my car (my car is black; you can sneeze and cause it to scratch). This eagle eyed woman from Rumson claimed to spot two new scratches on her bumper which was filled with many others. We pulled over and waited for the police. She made a veiled reference that she had just returned from the chiropractor (How ironic, I responded, so did I.) She was a registered nurse, but apparently chose to ignore my jaundice and my wan appearance.

She also took the opportunity to promote a NYC doctor's "nutritional treatment" strategy for attacking pancreatic cancer built around taking over a hundred supplements every day and enduring purgings that included coffee enemas (each supplement with convenient links to Amazon, BTW). She noted it might have been fate that we met, so that she could share this "potentially life saving" information with me. I thought it was bad timing that all my anti-nausea medications were at home.

The baby-faced patrolman who arrived on the scene probably hasn't had a first hand experience with a razor yet, but he was savvy enough to tell what was going on. I took blame for the accident, apologized, and after noting my own medical condition, emphasized that all I really wanted to do was to get home and go to bed. When he returned my paperwork, I said I'm fine with a ticket, but could he please give me one without traffic points. It was an unnecessary request. "I didn't give you a ticket," he said. "It was just a minor accident."

Sure enough, 24 hours later, my insurance company sent me a notice that a claim has been filed. I called the claims adjustor to give my side of the story, charmed her for thirty minutes, and then the conversation ended with her reminding me that I pay "big bucks" for coverage just to be protected in situations like these.

In sum, a woman living in a posh suburban community seeing an opportunity to take advantage of the system and get an old bumper replaced or maybe free medical care. It lacked both compassion and perspective, a sad reflection on what the rest of her life must be like.

Any sour feelings from that experience were quickly sweetened by Rebecca Barry, an author and spiritualist, who spoke a few days later at this weekend's TEDx conference on "Joy" at the Two River Theater in Red Bank. I had been invited, because my ode to marital miscommunication, "Hostage Situation," was being performed as part of the event (ironically BMW drivers are referenced in this play). I was feeling miserable, partly a reflection of my physical condition, and partly out of the frustration that I didn't have the energy to properly enjoy or network at this event. Barry's talk, which followed my play, was simply a happy accident.

Using the recent passing of her mother as an example, Rebecca told her audience about "Finding Joy in Death." She talked about her mother's good deeds and her acceptance of death with humor and grace. Rebecca filled her talk with warm anecdotes. In the final days, the family would gather in the mother's bedroom, sing songs, and break down in tears, only to have the mother finish the refrain (The spirit of these days are pleasantly reminiscent of a monologue I wrote for my play "Horseshoes." Maybe my dialogue is even more real than I give it credit.) Knowing her mother's life was nearing an end, Rebecca cherished the opportunity to spend time with her before she finally passed.

I made sure to reach out to Rebecca after her talk, to share my own story, and to express how much I had in common with her mother's attitude. She sensed a kindred spirit, wished me the best, "including my own journey going forward." Here's one example in which unexpectedly bumping into someone can be a positive.

MAY 28, 2022

We are on the cusp of summer and my pancreatic tumors in exile apparently prefer waterfront property; they have camped out around the bile ducts in my liver. The chemo police have tried to evict these intruders, but unfortunately, they continue to cause a lot of mischief. But they are also exposed and out in the open. If they want to do a little sun worshiping, I'm happy to oblige. They might get a bad sunburn if they are not careful.

After both liver stents collapsed, and I ended up in the hospital last month, I began asking a lot of questions about alternatives. The jaundice is gone and my liver's resilience continues to surprise everyone (it clearly doesn't want to end up on a plate with Fava beans). After weeks of nagging (I mean constructive conversation), I did manage to convince my oncologist that maybe radiation made sense to cause these tumors to shrink. Radiation seems to have destroyed my original pancreatic tumor. Maybe it could do the same level of damage with its brethren in my liver.

MSK is one of only two hospitals in the US with the tools and targeting strategy to inject higher than normal doses of radiation. The approach is fairly similar to giving the Ukrainians a lot of lethal toys to blow up Russian tanks.

Radiation treatments last about 90 seconds, but they pack a punch, usually making me both nauseous and tired. Since I have shrunk to my high school weight, I have no choice but to eat even if I don't feel like it (I've concluded that the first rule of eating when nauseous is never being afraid to vomit, which actually happens less often then you might think). I've finished the first week of sessions with two more weeks ahead of me, including another chemo treatment, my 59th if you are still counting at home.

My radiation oncologist seems pleased so far, which means the technicians are aiming their ray guns at the right place. That's good, because I've never been a fan of cooked liver anyway.

Soon I will reach the third anniversary of my original diagnosis, a rare milestone for my condition. A nurse in the medical team recently offered the best compliment that she could give. "You keep surprising us," she said.

JUNE 15, 2022

In the fall of 2019, I met three Colgate classmates in a bar in New York City--Kate Sweeney, Mark Herr, Blake Michaels, and Jim Joyce. We spent the time swapping old radio stories from our days at the college station back in the late 70s and 80s and Katie shared her plans for a reunion to recognize WRCU-FM's 70 anniversary the next year. I loved the idea, and pledged to be there.

Of course you would have had a hard time finding a Las Vegas bookie willing to post odds that I would fulfill my promise. I had been diagnosed with stage four pancreatic cancer a few months earlier. At best, my odds were 20% that I would survive 12 months. A June reunion would be cutting it close.

And then the pandemic hit, and the reunion went into hiatus for two years.

Last Friday morning, after finishing the 14th of 15 radiation sessions designed to pulverize a tumor lurking in my liver, I threw a bunch of stuff in my Volvo V60 XC and headed north. I was feeling weak and drained from treatments, forced to leave a day later than planned, and well aware that my physical state might resemble a well worn, damp dish rag after my four and a half hour trip was over.

It didn't matter. People with chronic illnesses like to talk about good and bad days. Unfortunately, that's too black and white. Most of my days fall in between, and each one forces you define how much you value the way you live your life. You balance the cost (discomfort, sluggishness, isolation) with the gain, which for the most part is the overwhelming absorption of energy that comes from socialization. People turn on a switch in me, and a cranky and corroded power grid wheezes and waxes as it jump starts. But those moments are priceless.

I also have the perfect car. Volvos are for life, and I doubt the Swedes really understand how true that phase is. My Volvo acts as my exoskeleton. I literally feel better when I drive in it. I don't think I could have made the round trip in any other vehicle.

The reunion was a double reunion. Members of the class of 81 were also there, to make up for our lost 40th reunion the year before. Among my friends to meet me, the incomparable Cathy Law, who served as my guardian angel, eager to drive me around when my neuropathic feet would no longer adapt to the hills of Colgate's Hamilton campus. Old friends came from everywhere. Hugs were not in short supply. They were the witnesses hanging on the sidelines of a marathon, cheering me on to reach the winning circle at the end of the race. My health made it difficult to experience quantity over the weekend; quality made up the difference.

The highpoint of the WRCU reunion was a special weekend radio show that ran over two days. Jim Joyce kicked it off, his voice still clear and forceful after 40 years. I would be the anchor that closed the event, so on Saturday afternoon, sitting in a gorgeously renovated radio control room, armed with a carefully curated list of eclectic selections, and accompanied by two students ready to lend a hand, I navigated my first radio show in decades.

Both students, including the current station GM, seemed impressed by the musical connectivity of my thirty minute jaunt. One, a self-confessed heavy metal enthusiast, admitted he wanted to check out "this Jade Bird" artist. They were delighted that I added an infamous one-hit wonder by the Buoys (ranked 32 on the Billboard 100 that same weekend in 1971) with "Timothy," a Rupert Holmes penned song about cannibalism.

I made sure to close the show with some subtle, positive vibes, the Velvet Underground's "Rock and Roll" ("You know, her life was saved by rock and roll.") and Collective Soul ("Let the word out/I've got to get out/Oh, I'm feeling better now.")

My music ended at 29:30. I hit the ID at the top of the hour. I still got it. ☺. Promise kept.

EPILOGUE

Mike's last posting was on June 15th. I imagine he stopped writing because the disease had worsen, had grown more resistant to treatment and he harnessed all his energy to fight it. The knowledge needed and the medical interventions required were as yet unknown to man. MSK did continue to monitor the progression of the disease until mid September when Mike was released from their care. I was with him at the time of his last meeting as the doctor who'd traveled his journey with him, hugged Mike and wished him well.

MSK offered the best suggestions they could to help Mike through his finally days. Would he prefer hospital treatment? Did he want Hospice care? How would he prefer his end to be?

Mike declined the suggestion of hospital care. He also declined a hospice facility. No, he would spend his remaining days at home, and seek help from Hospice care when needed. Mike still held the faith that this cancer was no match for his will. That somehow he would prove them wrong, both MSK and the cancer.

I remember about three weeks before Mike entered Hospice care, he called the human resources department of his company to request a three months sick leave. When the voice on the other end of the line asked if he thought he might have to extend it longer, he respond, " Yes, I might."

On the morning of September 23 Mike was taken to a facility in Holmdel that offered Hospice Care. The cancer was systematically destroying his liver, inhibiting oxygen from reaching his brain and impeding his ability to speak. This most articulate of men could no longer utter a word to the many friends and colleagues that streamed into his room to offer their love. How hard he tried, struggling to hold on to his vanishing world. As the end grew nearer, Mike lay gasping for breathe, his lungs starving for air. I sat bedside him holding his hand. " Tomorrow will be better," I whispered. Then suddenly, at about 3:30 p.m. on October the first, the harrowing gasps stopped.

I do not know what awaits us after our time on this earth is done. What I do know is that as long as Mike remains in the hearts and minds of those who knew and loved him, Mike Lives!

Lois Sockol, Mike's Mom

Printed in the United States
by Baker & Taylor Publisher Services